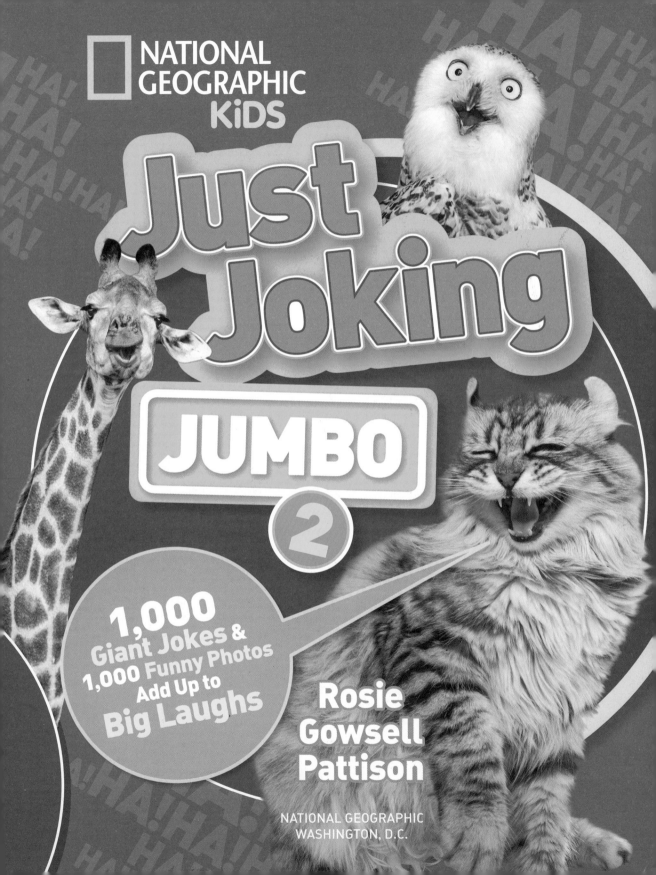

NATIONAL GEOGRAPHIC KIDS

Just Joking

JUMBO

2

1,000 Giant Jokes & 1,000 Funny Photos Add Up to Big Laughs

Rosie Gowsell Pattison

NATIONAL GEOGRAPHIC
WASHINGTON, D.C.

Contents

Tokay geckos use sticky hairlike structures on their toes to walk up walls.

CHAPTER 1

Preposterous Pets

ENGLISH

DEUTS

FRANÇAIS

ITALIA

ESPAÑO

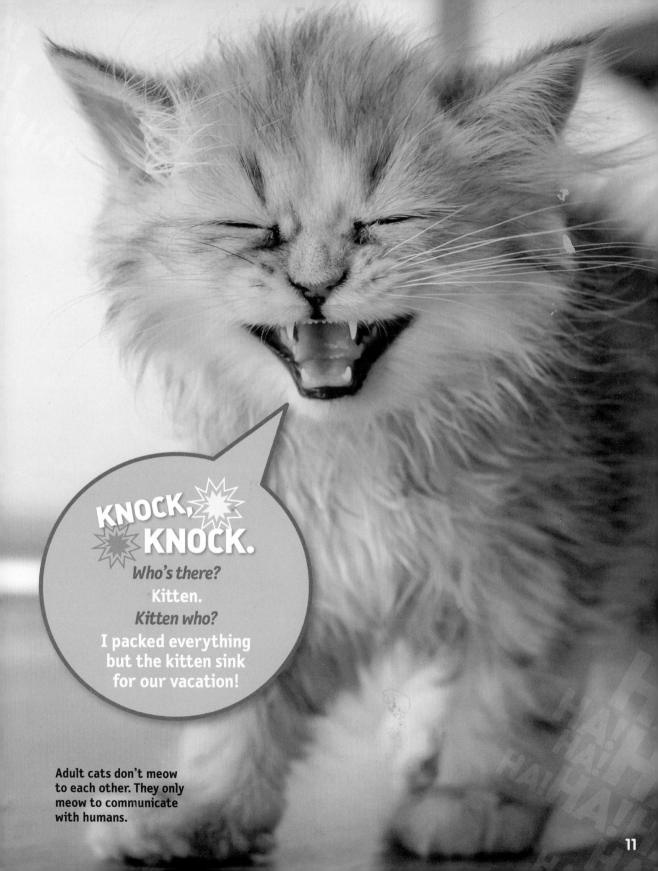

KNOCK, KNOCK.

Who's there?

Kitten.

Kitten who?

I packed everything but the kitten sink for our vacation!

Adult cats don't meow to each other. They only meow to communicate with humans.

KNOCK, KNOCK.

Who's there?

Whisker.

Whisker who?

Is Anne ready? I'm going to whisker away on a special trip.

Guinea pigs jump up and down when they are happy. This is often called popcorning.

I SAID, "DO YOU WANT TO COME OUT AND PLAY?"

Q Why don't cats like riddles?

A They find them purr-plexing.

Q What do you **get** if you **cross** a **magician** and a **dog?**

A A Labracadabrador.

LAUGHABLE LIST

FAVORITE DOG MOVIES:

- ☐ *Mary Puppins*
- ☐ *Bichon and the Beast*
- ☐ *Squeaky Toy Story*
- ☐ *Kung Fu Poodle*
- ☐ *Wizard of Paws*
- ☐ *Corgi With a Chance of Meatballs*

Q What happened to the cat that swallowed a ball of yarn?

A She had mittens.

Q What do you get if you cross a carnival ride and a weasel?

A A ferret wheel.

Q Why are **goldfish** easy to weigh?

A Because they have their own scales.

STEPHEN: Are you going to teach your dog to play soccer?
ANNA: Of course not, he's a boxer!

Q Why are books about frogs best sellers?

A Because they are quite ribbiting.

NAME Boss

FAVORITE ACTIVITY
Raiding the company fridge

FAVORITE TOY
Rubber-band balls

PET PEEVE
Forgetting my computer paws-word

The United States has the highest population of pet pooches. There are more than 70 million dogs living in the country.

THIS JOB MAKES ME DOGGONE TIRED.

WHEN I FETCHED THE STICK, I DIDN'T KNOW I'D BECOME THE BRANCH MANAGER!

I'M HAVING A RUFF TIME WITH THIS COMPUTER.

Q Why do cats like going to spas?

A They enjoy being pam-purred.

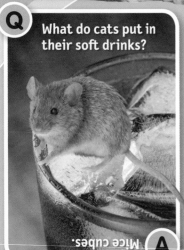

Q What do cats put in their soft drinks?

A Mice cubes.

IT'S ABOUT TIME SOMEONE LET THE CAT OUT OF THE BAG!

Q What's the difference between a **dog** and a **marine biologist?**

A One wags a tail and the other tags a whale.

JOSH:
Oh no! My bird escaped its cage!

DYLAN:
Looks like it used a crow-bar to escape.

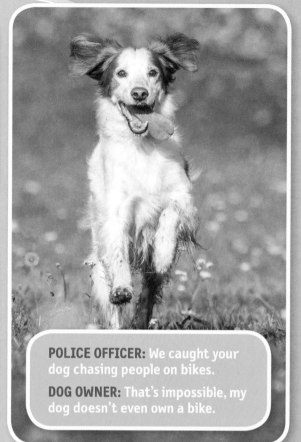

Did you know that **cats** were kept as pets in **ancient Egypt?**

They were considered sacred and associated with Bastet, a goddess who was half woman, half cat.

TONGUE TWISTER!

Say this fast three times:

A slimy snake slithered south to the sandy Sahara.

POLICE OFFICER: We caught your dog chasing people on bikes.

DOG OWNER: That's impossible, my dog doesn't even own a bike.

Q

Who do **dogs** hire to **design doghouses?**

A A bark-itect.

17

A BOY WALKS INTO A LIBRARY AND CHECKS OUT A BOOK.

Ten minutes later he returns it **and** gets another.

Ten minutes later he enters the library again, returns the second book, and takes out a third. **The librarian becomes suspicious and** follows the boy outside **where he sees him** talking to his pet frog.

The boy shows the book to the frog and says, "Okay, I'm getting tired of this. How about this book?"

And the frog replies, "Reddit, reddit."

KNOCK,
KNOCK.

Who's there?

Cook.

Cook who?

Stop making bird noises and open the door!

A parakeet's heart beats more than 300 times a minute.

What part of a bird isn't in the sky and can swim without getting wet?

The bird's shadow.

Q What do you get if you cross a turtle and a hedgehog?

A slowpoke. **A**

Q Where do mice park their boats?

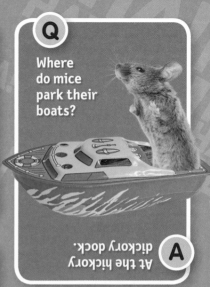

At the hickory dickory dock. **A**

BUS DRIVER: Where to?
FROG: I'm heading down to the pond. Mind if I catch a ride?
BUS DRIVER: Hop on!

Q What do cats listen to on their music players?

Mew-sic. **A**

Q What do rabbit surgeons perform?

Hop-erations. **A**

Q Why do Labradors like to wear hats?

Because they look quite fetching. **A**

Q **What do you call a dog standing in the snow?**

A chill dog. **A**

Q Why did the fish get embarrassed?

Because it saw the ocean's bottom. **A**

Goldfish don't have eyelids. That's why they are always staring at you.

KNOCK, KNOCK.

Who's there?
Chicken.
Chicken who?
I'd like to chicken to my room, please.

Q What is a **cat's** favorite **TV show?**

A Claw and Order.

Q What do you call a pet snake that can't sit still?

A Viper active.

I'M A PARTY ANIMAL!

Q Why did the teacher bring birdseed to class?

A She had a parrot-teacher conference.

Q What do you call a guinea pig with three eyes?

A Guinea piiig.

Q What kind of car do kittens drive?

A Cat-illacs.

Q What did the **schnauzer** say to the **hot dog bun?**

A "Are you a pure bred?"

PARAKEET 1: Is it hot out today?
PARAKEET 2: I didn't check the feather forecast.

Q How do **rabbits** travel?

A By hare-plane.

Q

What do you call an **extremely** happy **feline?**

Q

What do you get if you cross a pig and a parrot?

A A bird who hogs the conversation.

TEACHER: If I give you two cats and then another two cats, how many do you have?
SAM: Five.
TEACHER: How did you get five as an answer?
SAM: Because I already have a pet cat at home.

CAN YOU TURN THE HEAT UP?

CAN YOU TURN THE AIR-CONDITIONING ON?

Q What do you call a dog on a tanning bed?

SUN SCREEN 25 SPF

A A hot dog.

TONGUE TWISTER!

Say this fast three times:

Feathered finches flinch.

A

SHEEPDOG:
All 40 sheep are in the pen.

FARMER:
But we only have 38 sheep.

SHEEPDOG:
I know, but I rounded them up.

Did you know that **hairless dogs** have a **genetic defect** that causes their naked appearance?

These bare beauties are also completely odorless.

RIDDLE ME THIS

I'm **alive** without **air.** I'm always **drinking** but **never** thirsty. What am I?

A fish.

Q How do schnauzers celebrate the Fourth of July?

A They have a bark-becue.

Q

What do dogs eat while watching movies?

A Pup-corn.

NAME Mew-lissa

FAVORITE ACTIVITY
Meow-deling new fashions

DAILY GOALS
Tabby the best dressed

PET PEEVE
Smelly purr-fume

I THINK MY NEW LOOK IS GETTING A PAWSITIVE REACTION.

LOOKIN' GOOD, FELINE GOOD.

CATITUDE IS EVERYTHING.

A cat's nose has a unique pattern on it that is just as distinct as a human fingerprint.

27

Iguanas use their large tails to "punch" their attackers.

KNOCK, KNOCK.

Who's there?
Iguana.
Iguana who?
Iguana come inside!

If a **cat** can **jump** five feet high, why **can't** it jump **through** a window that is only **three feet high?**

The window is closed.

I FEEL LIKE I SHOULD BE THERE BY NOW. DID I PASS THE WATER BOTTLE ALREADY?

Q What did the frog order at the fast-food restaurant?

A A hoppy meal and flies.

Q Why do Shar-Peis have so many wrinkles?

A Because they're hard to iron.

Q Where does a poodle leave its car?

A In the barking lot.

Q What do you get if you cross a **dog** and a **vegetable?**

A A pug-tato.

Q When is it bad luck to see a black cat?

A When you're a mouse.

TING: Did you see the famous turtle over there?
LI: Wow, a real shell-ebrity!

Q What do you call a rodent with good aim?

A Accu-rat.

29

KNOCK, KNOCK.

Who's there?
Goat.
Goat who?
Goat to go, we're running late!

Goats can be taught to respond to their names and come when they are called.

WILL: Did you hear about the German shepherd on the hockey team?
KATE: He got a two-minute penalty for ruffing.

Q Why did the mother cat move her kittens away from the park?

A She didn't want to get caught littering.

Q Why is turtle wax so expensive?

A Because they have such small ears.

LAUGHABLE LIST

CAT EMPLOYMENT OPPORTUNITIES:

- ☐ Gravity tester (usually with your cup of cocoa)
- ☐ Keyboard warmer (while you are trying to use the computer)
- ☐ Fabric strength investigator (down the side of the couch)
- ☐ Feline scarf (Who needs to breathe?)
- ☐ Late-night opera singer (Why sleep when you can listen to a free live performance?)

POODLE: What movie do you want to watch?
PUG: *Bark to the Future*?
POODLE: I'd rather watch something scary.
PUG: How about *Jurassic Bark*?

Q How do **dogs** listen to **music?**

A On their subwoofers.

Q What do you give a dog with a fever?

A Mustard—it's the best thing for a hot dog.

SNAKE 1: Are we venomous?
SNAKE 2: I don't know, why?
SNAKE 1: Because I just bit my lip.

LOL PETS

The **LATIN NAME** name for **FERRET**, *Mustela putorius furo,* means "**smelly little thief.**"

DUKE, a Great Pyrenees, was elected **MAYOR** of a Minnesota, U.S.A., town for three terms.

Rats LAUGH and jump when they are tickled.

★ **LOST** ★

MADE A SLOW ESCAPE

A family in Brazil lost their pet tortoise and found it **30 YEARS LATER** still living in their house!

COSMO, AN **AFRICAN GRAY PARROT,** KNOWS **950 WORDS** AND TELLS **JOKES** TO HER OWNER FOR **PEANUTS.**

JUST ANOTHER DAY IN PARROT-DISE!

CHAPTER 2

Silly Science & Terrific Technology

The first known robot was a steam-powered bird created more than 2,300 years ago.

LAUGHABLE LIST

SIGNS YOU HAVE AN OLD COMPUTER:

☐ You have to crank a handle to start it.

☐ The screen is made by Etch-A-Sketch.

☐ It's connected to the Internet by a piece of string and a tin can.

☐ Your messaging app is a carrier pigeon.

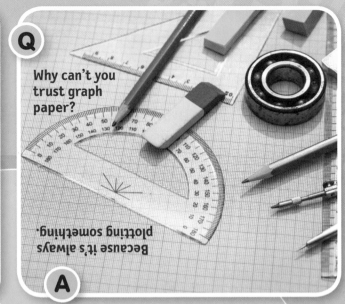

Q Why can't you trust graph paper?

A Because it's always plotting something.

RIZZO:
Hey, did you read that new book about helium?
SHERMAN:
Sure did, I couldn't put it down!

Q What do you get if you cross a soft drink and a robot?

A A can-droid.

Q Why did the **computer** keep **sneezing?**

A It had a virus.

Q What kind of snake is good at math?

$$\sqrt{4}=2$$

A An adder.

Q

What do you get
if you **cross**
baking soda and
an **android?**

A dough-bot.

A

I PREFER A COMPUTER WITH A MOUSE ...

Did you know that **Brazil** uses **cat face emojis** more than any other country in the **world?**

The cat with heart eyes is used the most of all the cat faces.

Q

What do you get
if you cross a
computer and a
dairy product?

Mac and cheese.

A

Q What did Earth say to the other planets?

A "You guys have no life."

Q What do you get if you cross helium and a monkey?

A A hot-air baboon.

RIDDLE ME THIS

You can **enter**, but you **can't come in.**

I can **give you space**, but no room.

I have **keys**, but **no lock.**

What am I?

A computer keyboard.

Q What does a robot use to shave?

A A laser blade.

CATHIE: I couldn't find the escape key on my computer.
DOUG: Did you get angry?
CATHIE: I lost control!

`Ctrl` `Cmd` `Alt`

Q Why was the **computer tired** when it **got home?**

A Because it had a hard drive.

Q Why did the germ cross the microscope?

A To get to the other slide.

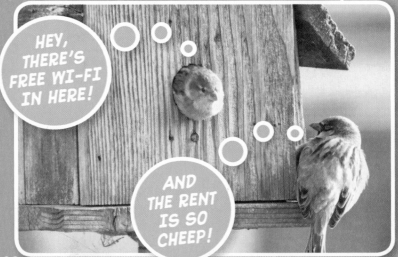

HEY, THERE'S FREE WI-FI IN HERE!

AND THE RENT IS SO CHEEP!

ELECTRICIAN'S BOSS: Wire you insulate?
ELECTRICIAN: Watt's it to you?

38

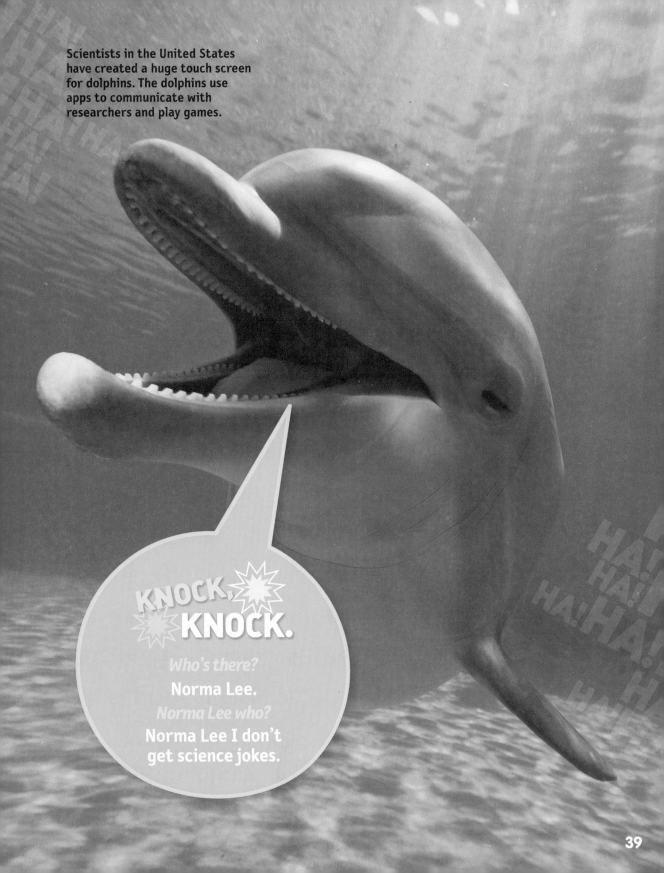

Scientists in the United States have created a huge touch screen for dolphins. The dolphins use apps to communicate with researchers and play games.

KNOCK, KNOCK.
Who's there?
Norma Lee.
Norma Lee who?
Norma Lee I don't get science jokes.

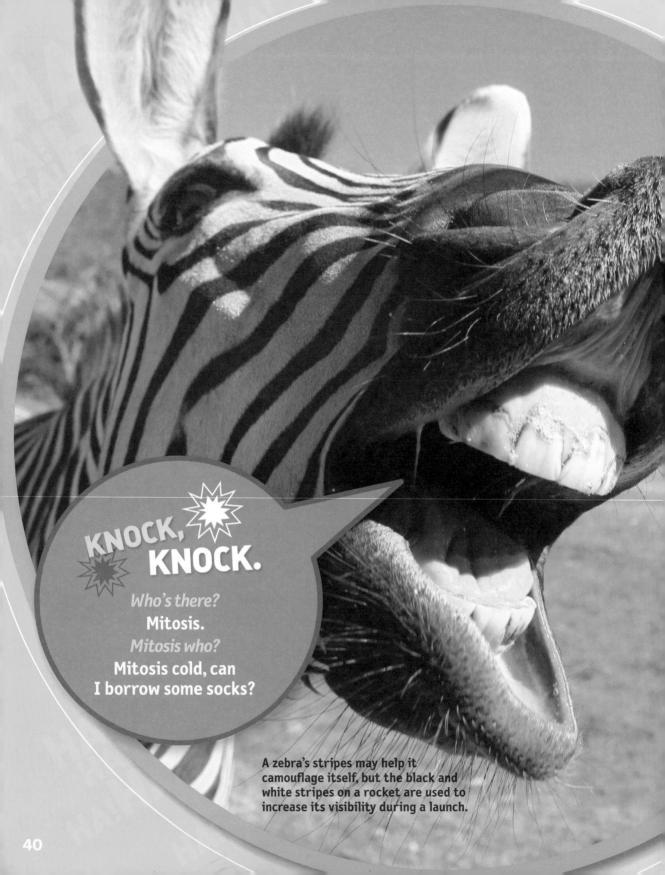

KNOCK, KNOCK.

Who's there?
Mitosis.
Mitosis who?
Mitosis cold, can
I borrow some socks?

A zebra's stripes may help it camouflage itself, but the black and white stripes on a rocket are used to increase its visibility during a launch.

Q Why did the **polar bear** call **tech support** from the North Pole?

A Because his computer was frozen.

Q What do you call a doctor that fixes websites?

A A URL-ologist.

Q What do you get if you cross a sheep and a hard drive?

A Computer ram.

Q What makes an astronaut's dog itchy?

A Lunar-ticks.

Q Why do computer programmers have terrible table manners?

A Because they take mega-bites.

Q Why did the **kid** sleep on a **battery?**

A She needed a power nap.

KYLIE: The light in here is bad.
JORJA: Maybe you should send it to prism.

Q Why shouldn't you let a skunk set up your Wi-Fi network?

A Because the service will stink.

Q Why did the robot cross the road?

A Because it was programmed by the chicken.

41

SAY WHAT?

NAME **Bunsen**

FAVORITE ACTIVITY
Hiding under the periodic table

FAVORITE TOY
Safety glasses

PET PEEVE
Over reactions

I ENJOY CHEMISTRY JOKES PERIODICALLY.

I HAVE ALL THE SOLUTIONS!

NEVER TRUST AN ATOM— THEY MAKE UP EVERYTHING.

I HAVE A LOT IN COMMON WITH MY COMPUTER ... WE BOTH HAVE MEGA-BITES!

SOLID, LIQUID, GAS ... THEY ALL MATTER.

Caimans are better suited for swimming than walking. They use their powerful tails to propel themselves through water.

KNOCK, KNOCK.

Who's there?

Data.

Data who?

Data pizza I smell? I sure am hungry!

RIDDLE ✷ ✷ ME THIS

What happens **once** in a minute, **twice** in a moment, but **never** in a thousand years?

The letter m.

Q What happened when the chemist tried to tell a joke?

A She didn't get a reaction.

TONY: Why did you put glasses on your cell phone?
LOUISE: Because it lost its contacts.

Did you know that **dogs** can be trained to alert **type 1 diabetics** when their blood sugar is low?

These detection dogs are specially trained to sniff out chemical changes in the body that happen when glucose levels drop.

YES, I'M A SCIENTIST ... I BET YOU WERE EXPECTING A LAB.

ASTRONOMER 1: What a beautiful sunset!
ASTRONOMER 2: Yeah, the Earth's rotation really makes my day.

Q What kind of shot do you give a sick car engine?

A A fuel injection.

Q Why couldn't the research assistant experiment with plants?

A Because he hadn't botany.

LAUGHABLE LIST

BOOKS BY ROBOT AUTHORS:

☐ *Artificial Intelligence and You* by Anne Droid

☐ *Don't Lose Your Head: A Guide to Keeping Yourself Together* by Si Borg

☐ *If I Only Had a Heart* by Otto Maton

☐ *How to Keep Your Insides Ticking* by Olata Gears

☐ *A Guide to Heavy Metal Music* by Metal Hedz

Q Why don't **computer programmers** like nature?

A There's too many bugs.

45

ONE DAY IN ROBOTICS CLASS, the teacher asked for a group of volunteers to test a batch of new robots. Four friends raised their hands. The teacher explained the plan: "Callie, you are operator one, Alex is operator two, Ling is operator three, and Rowan is operator four." They all grabbed their remote controls and got ready.

"These four robots are incredibly strong, and we are going to use them to carry this table across the room, but you MUST all move the robots together so we don't drop it," she said.

"Remember," the teacher said, "it is EXTREMELY important that all four of you hit the button on your remotes to move the robots forward at the same time, got it?"

"Got it!" the four friends replied. "Okay, kids," the teacher said. "Ready? One, two, three—go!" Everyone but Rowan pressed the button to move their robots forward. Suddenly, there was a loud crash, and the robots and the table collapsed into a jumbled, broken pile.

"Rowan!" the robotics teacher yelled. "Why didn't you move your robot?"

Rowan replied, "Because my number is four!"

KNOCK, KNOCK.

Who's there?
Art.
Art who?
Art2-D2.

Chimpanzees are one of the few animal species that make and use tools. They dig for grubs with sticks, smash open nuts with rocks, and even use leaves as sponges to soak up drinking water.

Q Why did the robot take a vacation?

A To recharge its batteries.

Q Why couldn't the computer take off its baseball hat?

A Because the caps lock was on.

Q What do you do with a **sick chemist**?

A Helium and hope you curium so you don't have to barium.

Q What do scientists use for breath freshener?

A Experi-mints.

Q How did the rocket lose its job at NASA?

A It was fired.

Q Why was there **thunder** and **lightning** in the lab?

A Because the scientists were brainstorming.

ROBOT: Can you help me loosen up? My neck is so stiff.
MASSAGE THERAPIST: Sure, I'll go get my screwdriver.

I'M THE NASTIEST COMPUTER BUG AROUND!

49

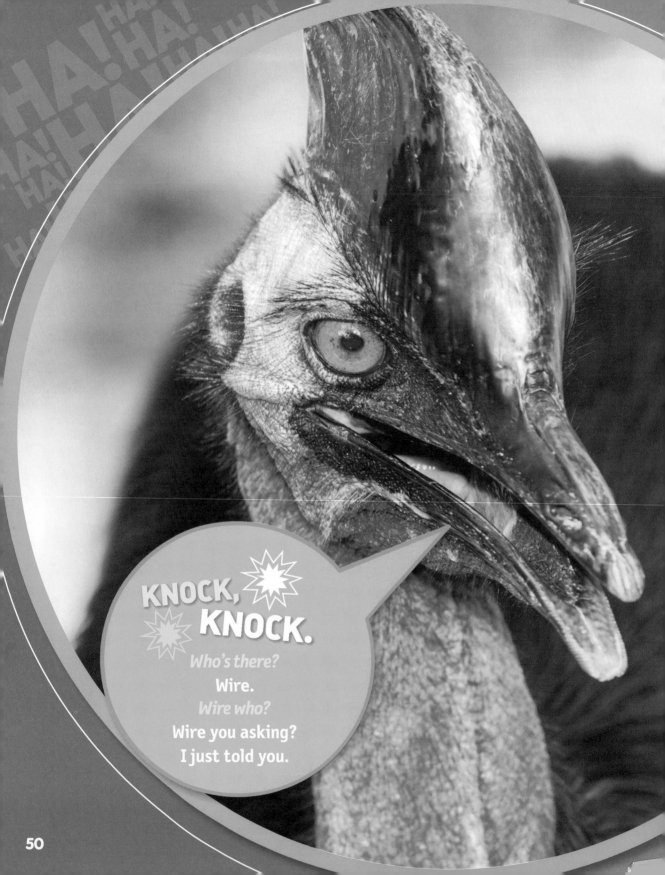

Q What do you get if you cross a robot and a gardener?

A Cutting-hedge technology.

COMPUTER 1: Can I borrow five dollars?
COMPUTER 2: Sorry, I used all my cache.

Q What kind of **garden** does a **droid** plant?

A A bot-tanical garden.

The cassowary, a large bird, has a long spike on each foot that it uses to defend itself.

EARS UP FOR A BETTER SIGNAL ... CAN YOU HEAR ME NOW?

LARISSA: I hear our science teacher is a vampire.
DYLAN: What?
LARISSA: She'll probably give us lots of blood tests.

Q What did the digital watch say to the grandfather clock?

A "Look, Pop! No hands!"

Q Why **couldn't** the **computer programmer sleep** at night?

A He had too much Java.

51

Q

What do you call dental x-rays?

A Tooth pics.

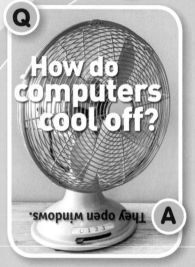

Q

How do computers cool off?

A They open windows.

VERY FUNNY, GUYS. WHO CHANGED MY SCREEN SAVER?

CHEMISTRY TEACHER: Who can tell me when the boiling point is reached?
STUDENT: When my mom sees my report card.

Q

Why didn't the computer talk to its parents about work?

A Because it makes its mother board.

Q What's a computer's favorite kind of dance?

A Disk-o.

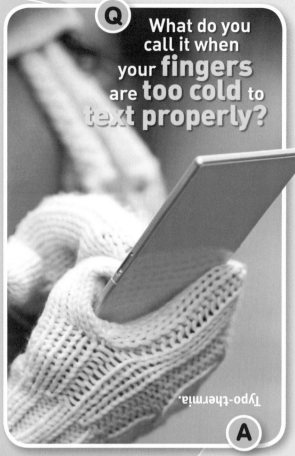

Q What do you call it when your **fingers** are **too cold** to **text properly?**

A Typo-thermia.

Did you know that **toque macaque monkeys** can have tails up to **24 inches** (61 cm) long?

These monkeys are named for their patches of hair that resemble brimless hats, called toques.

RIDDLE ME THIS

What starts out **tall,** but the **longer** it stands, the **shorter** it grows?

A candle.

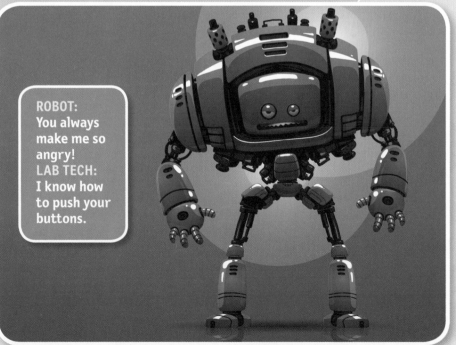

ROBOT: You always make me so angry!
LAB TECH: I know how to push your buttons.

SAY WHAT?

NAME Zippy

FAVORITE ACTIVITY
Trying to remember
my password

FAVORITE FOOD
Micro-chips

PET PEEVE
Caps lock

IF AT FIRST YOU DON'T SUCCEED, CALL IT VERSION 1.0.

KNOCK, KNOCK.

Who's there?

Ida.

Ida who?

Ida emailed but I have no Wi-Fi connection.

IS THE INTERNET SLOW TODAY, OR IS IT JUST ME?

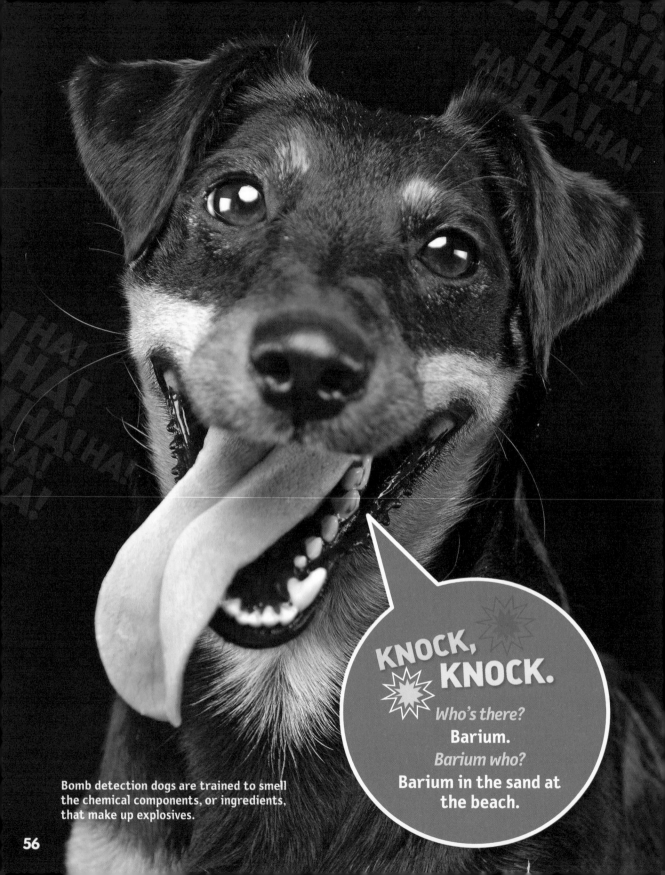

Bomb detection dogs are trained to smell the chemical components, or ingredients, that make up explosives.

KNOCK, KNOCK.

Who's there?
Barium.
Barium who?
Barium in the sand at the beach.

Q What do **computers** **eat** for a **snack?**

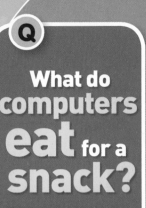

A Microchips.

Q If there is H$_2$O on the inside of the fire hydrant, what is on the outside?

A K9P.

Q What kind of math does a bird do?

A Owl-gebra.

Q What is the first thing the lumberjack did with his new computer?

A He logged in.

Q Why are chemists great at solving problems?

A Because they have all the solutions.

SCIENCE TEACHER: I'd like to have a large whiteboard installed in my classroom.

PRINCIPAL: Sure, but what's so great about whiteboards?

SCIENCE TEACHER: They're remarkable!

Q How do **cars greet** each other?

A With their hi-beams.

Q What do **computers** do on **first dates?**

A Grab a byte.

Q **How** can you tell if a **cat** has been using your **computer?**

A There's teeth marks on your mouse.

KNOCK, KNOCK.

Who's there?
Argon.
Argon who?
All of my good jokes argon.

Shetland ponies are only about 42 inches (107 cm) tall.

58

Q

What is the most important rule in a chemistry lab?

A Don't lick the spoon.

Q

Did you hear about the wooden car with the wooden engine?

A It wooden go.

SCIENTIST: I'm thinking about getting a dog. Any suggestions?
ASSISTANT: How about a Lab?

Q

How do locomotives hear?

A With their engine-ears.

Q

What did the biologist buy at the high-end boutique?

A Designer genes.

Q

What **do you get** if **you cross a lifeguard** and a **computer?**

A A screen saver.

Q

What did one **magnet** say to the **other?**

A I find you very attractive.

59

LOL

SCIENCE & TECHNOLOGY

A group of **programmers** have created a **COMPUTER CODE** that can "**write**" a 50,000 word novel.

In 2015, the Oxford Dictionary's **WORD** of the **YEAR** was the "**Face with Tears of Joy**" **emoji**.

Japanese researchers built a **HUMANOID ROBOT** that can **laugh** and **smile**.

In 1950, an American sound engineer created the **LAUGH TRACK,** a recording of **audience laughter,** to be used during **COMEDY TV SHOWS** that were recorded without **live audiences.** It is still **used** today.

THERE'S A **ROBOT** PROGRAMMED TO PERFORM ORIGINAL STAND-UP COMEDY ROUTINES. IT WILL CHANGE OR REVISE THE **JOKES** IT TELLS BASED ON **AUDIENCE** REACTIONS.

I TOOK A SICK DAY BECAUSE I HAD A VIRUS.

CHAPTER 3

Side-splittingly Spooky

HA!HA!HA!HA!
HA!HA!HA!
HA!HA!
HA!HA!

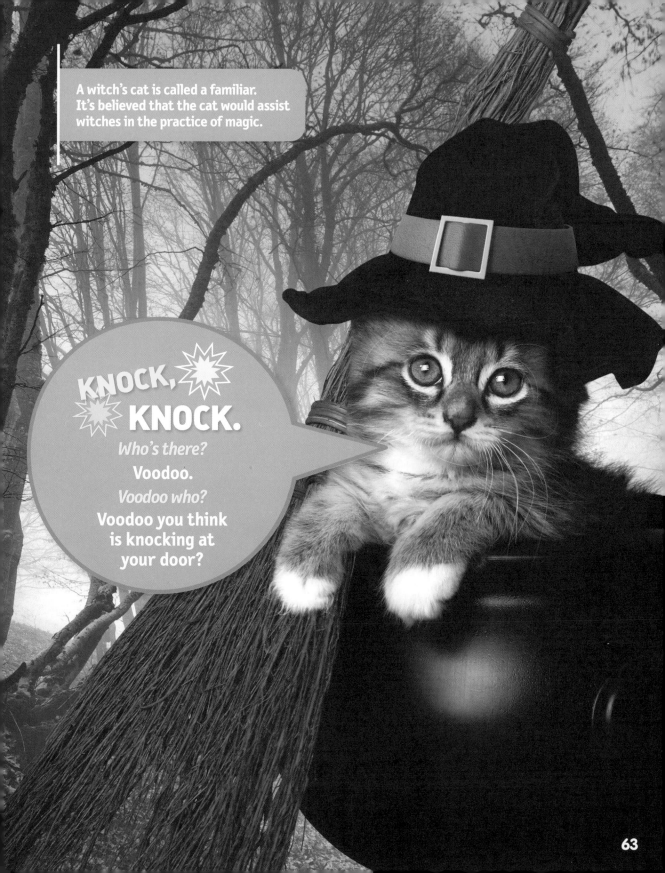

A witch's cat is called a familiar. It's believed that the cat would assist witches in the practice of magic.

KNOCK, KNOCK.
Who's there?
Voodoo.
Voodoo who?
Voodoo you think is knocking at your door?

MOM:
I'm going to tell you a story about a haunted refrigerator.
DAUGHTER:
That sounds chilling!

Q What do you get if you cross a Scottish monster and a German cheese?

A The Loch Ness Muenster.

Q What do spirits send home while on vacation?

WISH YOU WERE HERE!

A Ghost-cards.

Q Why can't **skeletons** play church **music?**

A Because they don't have organs.

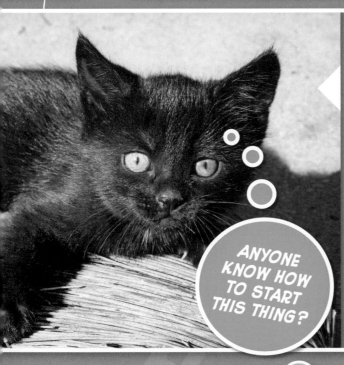

Did you know that there are both **good** and **bad** superstitions around **black cats?**

In Japan, they are believed to bring good luck.

ANYONE KNOW HOW TO START THIS THING?

Q What is a **zombie's** favorite **hairstyle?**

A Deadlocks.

DAD: I don't want to be buried in a cemetery.
SON: Why not?
DAD: I'm not dead yet!

Q Where do **vampires** keep their **Easter eggs?**

A In their Easter caskets.

Q How does the Abominable Snowman build his house?

A Igloos it together.

Q How does a skeleton call his friends?

A On the tele-bone.

Q What position does a ghost play on a soccer team?

A Ghoul-keeper.

Q Why does **Dracula annoy his friends?**

A Because he's a pain in the neck.

Q Why won't you find cattle at scary movies?

A Because they are cow-ards.

RIDDLE ☀ ME THIS

It comes in only one color, but many different sizes. It lives where there's light but will die in the rain. What is it?

Your shadow.

Q What position does the invisible man play on his hockey team?

A No one knows.

Q What kind of shoes does a ghost wear?

A Boooots.

DRACULA: I'd like to write a book about my life.
GHOUL: Maybe you should hire a ghostwriter.
DRACULA: I'm hoping it will be a best seller.
GHOUL: Then you can start a fang club!

Some people once believed that dun-colored (brown or gray) duck eggs were bad luck.

KNOCK, KNOCK.
Who's there?
Witches.
Witches who?
Witches the way home? I think I'm lost.

67

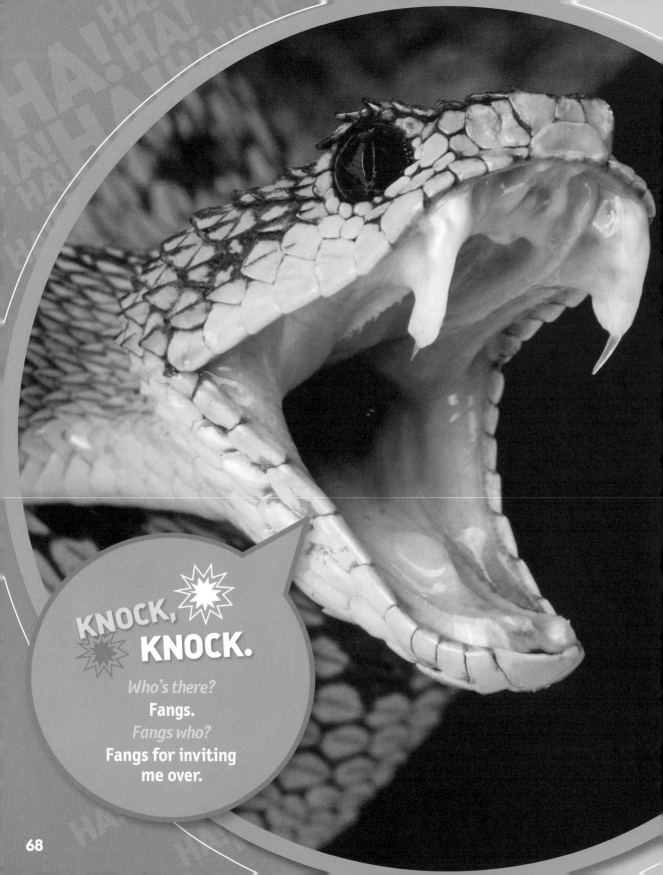

Q Who do monsters buy cookies from?

A The Ghoul Scouts.

Q What do **witches** use to **style** their **hair?**

A Scare spray.

PATIENT: I think I was bitten by a vampire.
DOCTOR: Take a drink of water.
PATIENT: Will it make me better?
DOCTOR: No, but I'll be able to see if your neck leaks.

RIDDLE ☀ ☀ ME THIS

Three men were hunting **Bigfoot** when it started to rain. Only **two** of them got their **hair wet.** How is that possible?

The third man was bald.

Snakes can regrow their fangs quickly when they break or wear out. Some species have up to six fangs developing in their gums at one time.

Q What do **vampires** take for a **sore throat?**

A Coffin drops.

Q Why did the witches' team lose the baseball game?

A Their bats flew away.

Q What has large fangs and says "baa"?

A A ram-pire.

Q What do you call a hot dog bun with nothing inside it?

A A hollow-weenie.

NAME **The Flappy Family**

FAVORITE ACTIVITY **Hanging with our friends**

FAVORITE SUPERHERO **Batman**

PET PEEVE **Sunny days**

YOU'RE JUST MY TYPE ... O-NEGATIVE!

I PUT WHIPPED SCREAM ON MY SUNDAES.

I STOPPED IN AT MY FRIEND'S PLACE FOR A BITE OF DINNER. IT WAS FANG-TASTIC!

Bats can eat up to 1,200 mosquitoes in one hour.

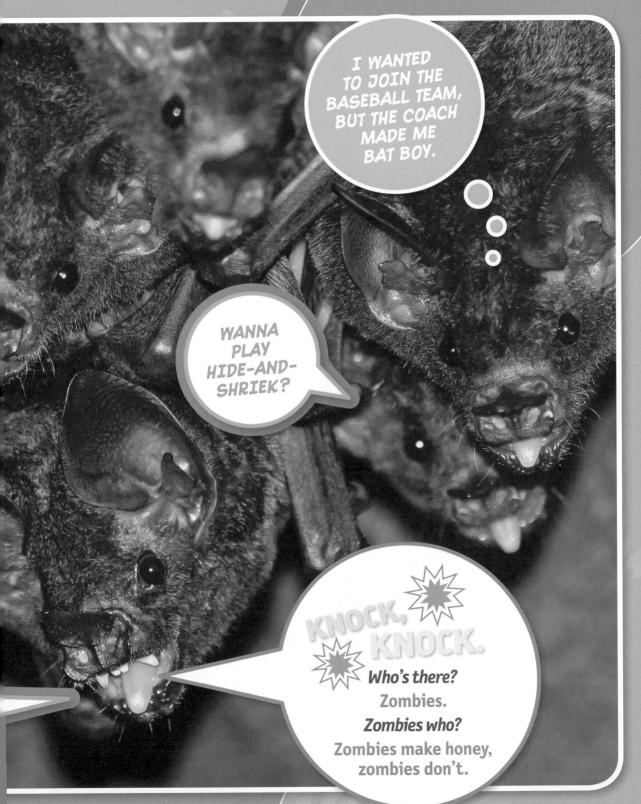

71

R.I.P.
Al B. Bach

AUTHOR: I think I have writer's block.
EDITOR: Why don't you head to the cemetery? There's lots of plots there.

R.I.P.
Ricky D. Bones

LAUGHABLE LIST

NOT VERY SCARY MONSTERS:

- ☐ The Toe Tickler
- ☐ Abominable Sno-Kone
- ☐ The Sock-less Monster
- ☐ Soup-acabra

CAH! CAH ... OR IS THAT A TRUCK?

GHOUL: Why do you think we get along so well?
DEMON: Because demons are a ghouls best friend!

Q

What string instrument does a ghost play?

Q

What time is it when Godzilla sits on your bed?

A Time to get a new bed.

Q

What is **Bigfoot's** favorite **month?**

WARNING!

PLEASE DO NOT FEED THE SASQUATCH

A Oc-toe-ber.

Did you know that **crows** are **extremely intelligent birds** with amazing problem-solving **skills?**

Researchers have found that crows are able to recognize the faces of humans they have met before.

What runs around a haunted house but doesn't move?

A fence.

A spook-ulele.

Q

What did the ghost cook for his dinner party?

A Spook-etti and ghoulash.

73

DRACULA WAS SITTING AT HOME ONE DAY WHEN THE DOORBELL RANG. When he opened the door, a six-foot (1.8-m)-tall cockroach kicked him in the shins and ran away.

The next evening, there was a knock at the door. When he opened it, there was the same cockroach. Before Dracula could say anything, the cockroach poked him in the eye and ran away.

On the third evening, the cockroach broke into Dracula's house, smashed his TV, knocked over his plants, and hit Dracula on the head. Dracula crawled to the phone and dialed 911. At the hospital, the doctor was very concerned.

"Can you tell me what happened?" the doctor asked. Dracula told him the events of the last three nights.

"Yes, it's not surprising," the doctor said. "There's definitely a nasty bug going around."

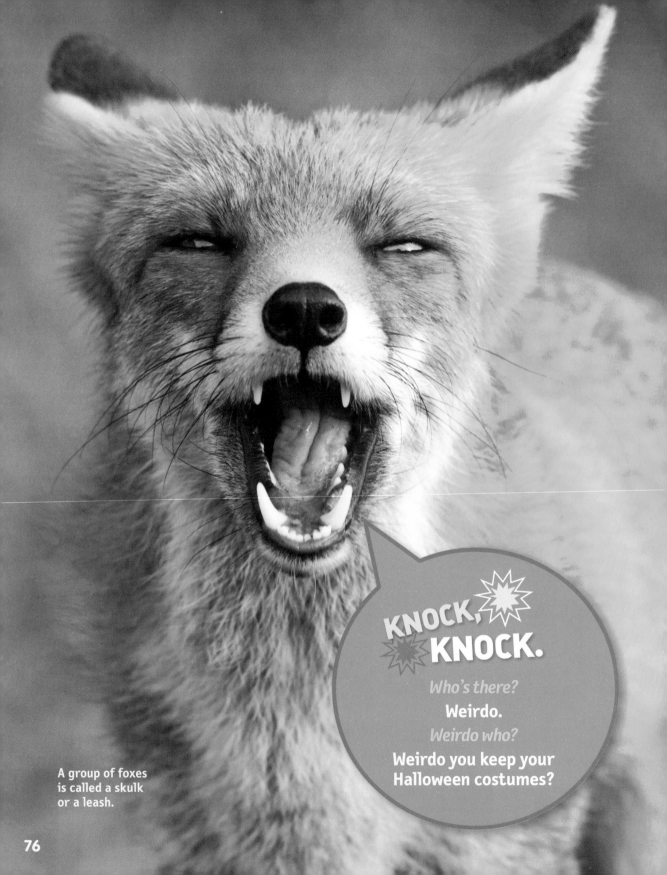

A group of foxes is called a skulk or a leash.

KNOCK, KNOCK.

Who's there?

Weirdo.

Weirdo who?

Weirdo you keep your Halloween costumes?

Say this fast three times:

Haunted houses house *horrifying* haunts.

Q What does Dracula take when he is sick?

A Bite-amins.

LAUGHABLE LIST

TERRIBLE
HALLOWEEN TREATS:

☐ Scabby Taffy—pick your favorite flavor.

☐ Taran-chew-las—bite into them before they bite you.

☐ Pickled Pumpkin Guts— eat till you bust a gut!

☐ Furry Fun Dip—now with 10 percent more hair!

Q Which is a witch's favorite subject?

A Spelling.

Q What do you call a monster with no neck?

A The Lost Neck Monster.

Q Why was the werewolf banned from the butcher shop?

A He was caught chop-lifting.

Q What do ghosts bring their dates?

A A boo-quet of flowers.

VAMPIRE 1:
What did you think of that Dracula movie?
VAMPIRE 2:
It was fang-tastic!

SSSHH ... DID YOU HEAR THAT NOISE?

I'M SCARED ... I'M GOING TO SQUEAL.

I DON'T KNOW WHY I LOST MY JOB AT THE PETTING ZOO.

MONSTER 1: What is your son studying at medical school?
MONSTER 2: Nothing, they're studying him!

Q Why did the vampire go to the library?

A He was looking for a book to sink his teeth into.

Orange tabby cats are almost always male.

Q What happened when the werewolf swallowed a clock?

A He got ticks.

GARY: Did you hear that the invisible man married the invisible woman and had a baby?
NICO: Is the baby cute?
GARY: She's nothing to look at.

Q Where does a **ghoul water-ski?**
A On Lake Eerie.

Q Why do **zombies** make **great** employees?

Q What do **ghosts** use to clean their **hair?**
A Sham-boo!

Q What is a scarecrow's favorite fruit?

A Straw-berries.

A Because they are dead-icated.

OPTOMETRIST: Your eyesight is terrible.

GHOST: What can I do about it?

OPTOMETRIST: I can fit you with a pair of spook-tacles.

Q What's big and **HAIRY** and has three wheels?

A A Bigfoot on a tricycle.

RIDDLE ✴ ME THIS

I dig tiny holes and **fill them** with **silver** or **gold**. I also can build **bridges of silver** and **crowns of gold**. Sooner or later **everyone** sees me, but most are afraid of me. **Who am I?**

The dentist.

HE'S RIGHT BEHIND ME, ISN'T HE?

Did you know that there is a **species of frog** that will **break its own bones** to create **claws** in order to protect itself?

The end result looks like a cat's claw protruding from the frog's toes.

Q What do **witches** order at **fancy** hotels?

A Broom service.

Q What kind of **cereal** does a **yeti** eat?

A Snowflakes.

Q What kind of lock does a ghost have on its front door?

A A dead bolt.

WAITER ON CRUISE SHIP: Would you like to see a menu, sir?

WEREWOLF: No thanks, just bring me the passenger list.

Q Who won the skeleton beauty pageant?

A Nobody.

Q What does a **monster** put in its **coffee?**

A Scream and sugar.

SAY WHAT?

GHOST DOGS ARE TERRIER-FYING!

NAMES Trick and Treat

FAVORITE ACTIVITY
Shopping at the ghost-ery store

FAVORITE TOY
Our owner's old boooooo-ts

PET PEEVE
Laundry day

In some parts of the world, it was believed that phantom dogs guarded entries to the underworld, and you would die if you looked directly at one.

83

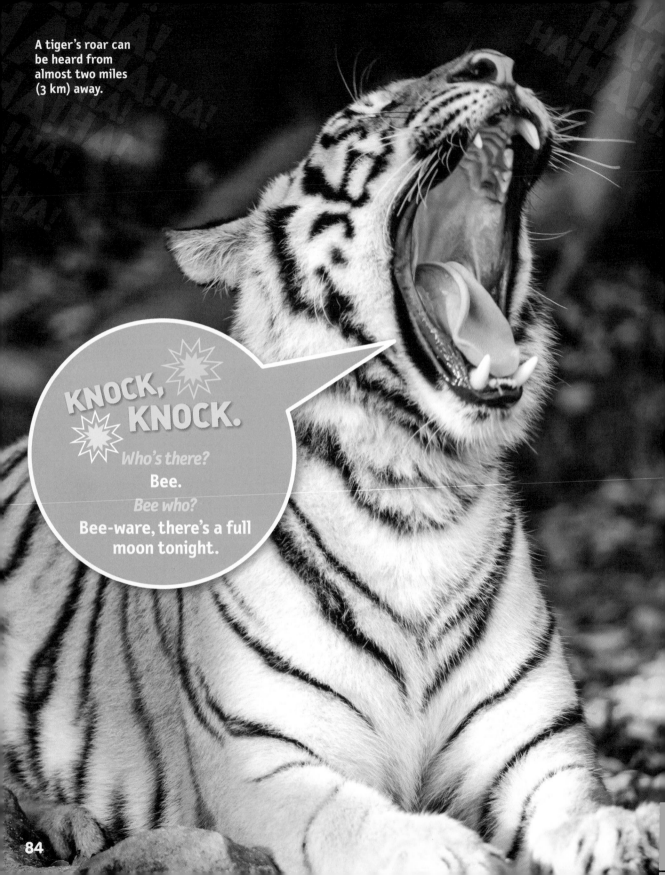

A tiger's roar can be heard from almost two miles (3 km) away.

KNOCK, KNOCK.

Who's there?

Bee.

Bee who?

Bee-ware, there's a full moon tonight.

Q What do you call a **zombie** that is pressing your **doorbell?**

A A dead ringer.

KNOW ANY GOOD DENTISTS?

Q How did the scarecrow fix the hole in his pants?

A With a pumpkin patch.

Q What do you get if you cross a witch with Rice Krispies?

A Snap, cackle, and pop!

WAITER: Welcome to Soul Food, may I take your order?
GHOST: I'll have the boo-logna sandwich.

Q What **quacks** and has **feathers** and **fangs?**

A Count Duckula.

Q What do you call a large Irish spider?

A Paddy longlegs.

Q What's as sharp as a vampire's fang?

A The other fang.

Q What has **one eye, purple** spots, prickles, and **eats rocks?**

A A one-eyed, purple-spotted, prickled, rock-eater.

85

KNOCK, **KNOCK.**

Who's there?

Ooze.

Ooze who?

Ooze that monster creeping up on you?!

Green crested lizards are bright green but can turn brown when threatened.

Q What kind of **makeup** do **zombie models** wear?

A Ma-scare-a.

Q What time do man-eating monsters wake up?

A Ate o'clock.

Q Which monster plays the best tricks on his friends?

A Prank-enstein.

Q Which **ghost** is the best **dancer?**

A The boogie man.

Q How does a girl vampire flirt with her boyfriend?

A She bats her eyes.

Q What do you call **two spiders** who just got **married?**

A Newly-webs.

Q What kind of vehicle does Bigfoot drive?

A A monster truck.

KID: Trick or treat!
WOMAN: What are you supposed to be?
KID: A werewolf.
WOMAN: But you aren't wearing a costume.
KID: Well, it isn't a full moon yet.

87

LOL SPOOKY

A **COMEDY CLUB** in Hollywood, California, U.S.A., is reportedly **haunted** by the **GHOST** of a **COMEDIAN** who was banned from performing there.

Disneyland's **HAUNTED MANSION** ride in California, U.S.A., is reported to have **999 HAPPY HAUNTS** residing in it.

The **DEOGEN** is a **GHOST** said to **haunt a forest** in Belgium. It appears as a **GREENISH FOG** and sounds like a **child laughing.**

In Brazil it is believed that a **BLACK CAT** walking **toward you** brings good luck, but if it walks away, it will **TAKE** your good luck with it.

EVERY YEAR, A PARK IN NEW YORK CITY HOSTS AN ANNUAL **HALLOWEEN PET PARADE** WHERE **HUNDREDS OF DOGS** IN **COSTUMES** COMPETE IN A **RUNWAY SHOW** TO WIN PRIZES.

ZOLTAR

I SEE TREATS IN YOUR FUTURE.

CHAPTER 4

Absurd Adventures

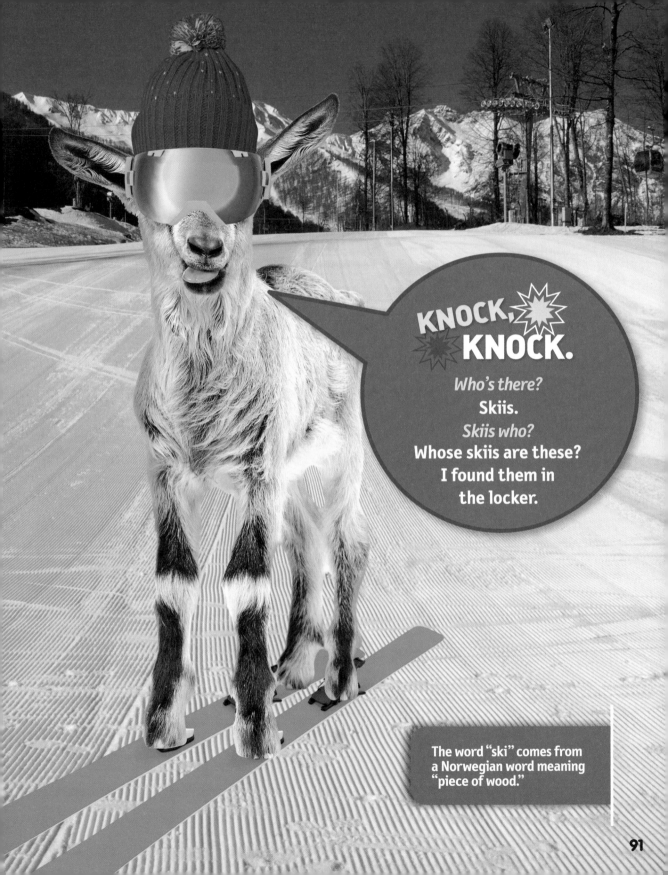

KNOCK, KNOCK.

Who's there?
Skiis.
Skiis who?
Whose skiis are these?
I found them in
the locker.

The word "ski" comes from
a Norwegian word meaning
"piece of wood."

RIDDLE ✹ ME THIS

What's **harder** to **catch** the **more** that you **run?**

Your breath.

Q

What do they serve for lunch at martial arts camp?

Kung food. **A**

Q

What do you call an elephant in a kayak?

Stuck. **A**

Q

Why did the opera singer go sailing?

She wanted to hit the high C's. **A**

Did you know that your **cat** prefers to drink from **running water** sources like **faucets** more than still water sources like **its bowl?**

Some domestic cat breeds, like the Turkish Van, love to swim.

GINGERBREAD MAN: I hurt my knee while rock climbing today.
GINGERBREAD WOMAN: Have you tried icing it?
GINGERBREAD MAN: Not yet, I've just been using a candy cane.

Q Why are **gymnasts** the best **friends?**

A Because they always bend over backward for people.

Q Why do **scuba divers** fall off the boat **backward** to **enter** the water?

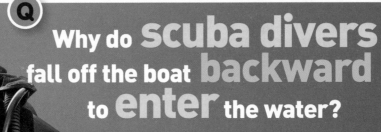

A Because if they fell forward, they'd fall in the boat.

IT'S A PAW-SITIVELY CLAW-SOME DAY FOR SAILING.

Q What do pine trees wear to the lake?

A Swimming trunks.

Q What did the cyclist eat when he was in last place?

A Ketchup.

CAMP LEADER: Good morning, campers!
CAMPER: Shhhhh, please don't talk so loud!
CAMP LEADER: Oh! Sorry ... what's wrong?
CAMPER: I've got a sleeping bag, and I don't want to wake it up.

Q Why do puppies make the best kayakers?

A Because they are natural dog paddlers.

BAA, I HERD YOU WERE EASY TO BLEAT.

EWE DON'T STAND A CHANCE AGAINST ME IN THIS RACE.

Q What do you call **four bullfighters** that fall in **quicksand?**

A Quattro sinko.

Q What's the hardest part about skydiving?

A The ground.

Q Why isn't **tanning** a competitive **sport?**

A Because you can only get bronze.

KATE: Are you all ready for our mountain climbing trip?
MICHAELA: Yep, I'm in peak condition!

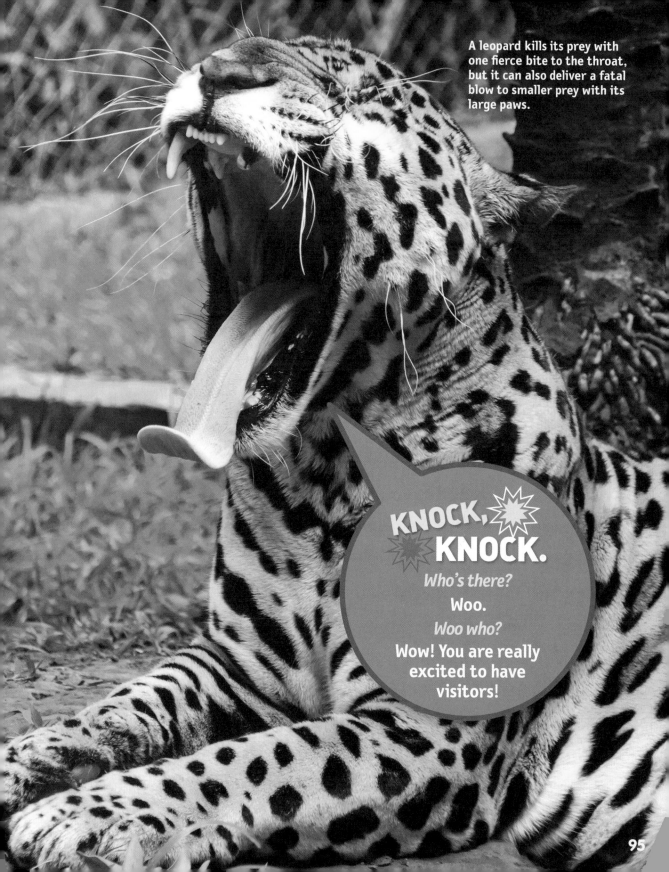

A leopard kills its prey with one fierce bite to the throat, but it can also deliver a fatal blow to smaller prey with its large paws.

KNOCK, KNOCK.

Who's there?

Woo.

Woo who?

Wow! You are really excited to have visitors!

Q Why did the chicken cross the basketball court?

A Because the ref called a foul.

Q What do you get if you cross a fishing lure and an old gym sock?

A A hook, line, and stinker.

Q What do **archers** wear when they want to get **dressed up?**

A Bow ties.

LAUGHABLE LIST

CRAZY CAMPSITES:

☐ **Camp Soggy Bottom**— leakiest tents around!

☐ **Camp Eyedont Wannago**— voted least popular camp since 2006.

☐ **Camp Itchy**—we have four types of bedbugs!

☐ **Camp Rickety Pines**—you don't want to set your tent up under those trees.

Q What happens to skydivers when it rains?

A They get wet.

RIDDLE ME THIS

Two fathers and two sons go fishing, but there are only three people in the boat. How is this possible?

It was a grandfather, a father, and a son on the fishing trip.

JIM: Want to go rock climbing with me?
ELLEN: I would if I was boulder.

A puffin's beak changes color during the year. It's bright orange in the spring and changes to a dull gray in the winter.

WE'RE NATURAL-BORN SNORKELERS!

Q What's big, scary, and carries binoculars?

A A monster on safari.

NAME Otto

FAVORITE ACTIVITY
Floating with my significant otter

FAVORITE FOOD
Seafood

PET PEEVE
Hard-to-catch fish

I OTTER LEAVE FOR MY TRIP NOW.

IS THE RIVER BANK STILL OPEN? I NEED SOME CASH.

I'M GOING TO HAVE AN OTTER-LY GREAT VACATION!

River otters are playful adventure-seekers. They are often spotted diving up to 60 feet (18 m) underwater, belly flopping into rivers, or sliding down muddy hills on their tummies.

Q What do you get if you cross a **musical instrument** and a **snorkeler?**

A A tuba diver.

Q What do you call a girl hanging onto a basketball hoop?

A Annette.

THOSE SKATEBOARDING LESSONS ARE REALLY PAYING OFF!

Q Why is **basketball** such a **messy** sport?

A Because you dribble on the floor.

GUIDE: If you look to your left, you'll see a talking giraffe.
TOURIST: Wow! He's really talking up a storm!
GUIDE: Yes, he's giving a speech on the solar system but it's kind of hard to hear.
TOURIST: Oh well, it's way over my head anyway.

Q

Why aren't sumo wrestlers friends with race car drivers?

A Because they move in different circles.

Did you know that many **dogs** have learned to perform human sports like **skateboarding, surfing,** and **water-skiing?**

Flyball is a dog sport where four pooches work together to complete a relay obstacle course.

RIDDLE ✷ ✷ ME THIS

A man rode into the **Grand Canyon** for a camping tour on **Friday,** stayed for two nights, and **left** on **Friday.** How is this possible?

His mule's name was Friday.

What activity does the sun enjoy?

Q

Solar-blading.

A

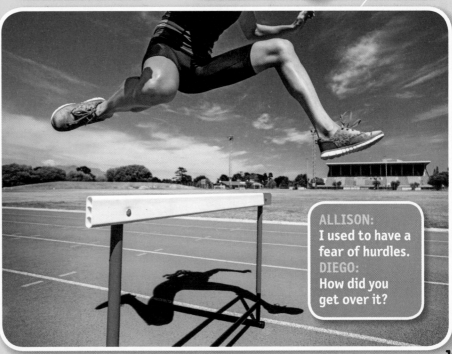

ALLISON: I used to have a fear of hurdles.
DIEGO: How did you get over it?

TINA AND LOUISE WERE HIKING ON A SAVANNA WHEN TINA YELLED, "WOW! DID YOU SEE THAT OSTRICH RUN BY?"

"Uh ... no, I didn't," Louise said sheepishly.

"What?" Tina says, "It was huge— I can't believe you missed it!"

They hiked on and a few minutes later, Tina exclaimed, "Wow! That was amazing! Did you see that elephant? It just crossed our path on the trail ahead."

Embarrassed, Louise replied, "Oh … no, I didn't see it."

"I can't believe you missed it," Tina says. Thirty seconds later, Tina looked back and at Louise and yelled, "Whoa! Did you see that?"

Louise was annoyed at this point. "Yes, I did!" she lied.

Tina replied, "Then why did you step in it?"

A gorilla's hands and feet are a lot like a human's—they have thumbs and big toes that can grasp and hold on to things.

Q What kind of workouts do chickens follow?

A Egg-cersize routines.

Q What kind of money do fishermen make?

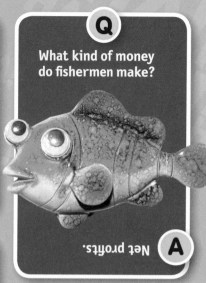

A Net profits.

Q Which highway does a tree take on a road trip?

A Root 66.

Q What do you do if you go on safari and a lion wants to sleep in your tent?

A Sleep somewhere else.

Q Where do monkeys get all their gossip?

A Through the apevine.

RIKU: Are you going to watch the fishing competition today?
KEVIN: Is it online?
RIKU: Yes, but I can't get a good stream.

Q What's worse than having a snake in your sleeping bag?

A Two snakes in your sleeping bag.

I WANTED TO GO WHITE WATER RAFTING BUT FORGOT MY RAFT.

105

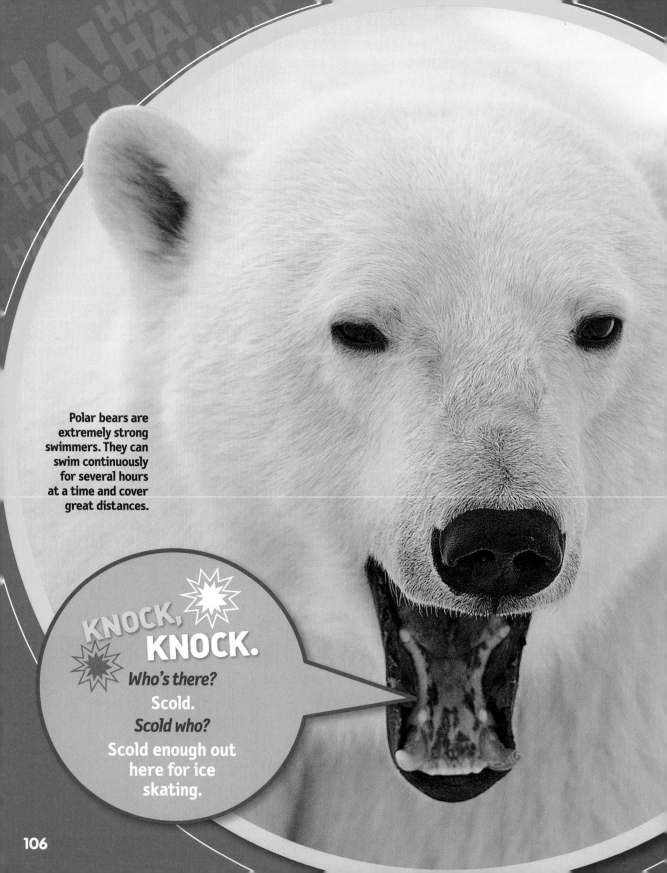

Polar bears are extremely strong swimmers. They can swim continuously for several hours at a time and cover great distances.

KNOCK, KNOCK.

Who's there?

Scold.

Scold who?

Scold enough out here for ice skating.

Q Why did the invisible man turn down a free kayaking trip?

A He just couldn't see himself doing it.

Q How can you tell if the tree you are camping under is a dogwood?

A By the bark.

Q When does the **Golden Gate Bridge** get **angry?**

A When someone crosses it.

FISHERMAN 1: Is this river good for fish?
FISHERMAN 2: It must be, I can't get any of them to leave!

Q Why did the **kayaker** cross the **Atlantic?**

A To get to the other tide.

Q Why did the cookie go to the doctor after hiking?

A Because it was feeling crumby.

Q Which **race** is never **run?**

A A swimming race.

Q How did the lobster take a tour of the Grand Canyon?

A By shell-icopter.

107

SKIER 1: I can't find my sister; she was just near the chairlift.
SKIER 2: She's gondola top of the mountain.

Q How do **fleas** travel?

A They go itch-hiking.

SURE, I ENJOYED THE CLIMB UP, BUT HOW DO WE GET DOWN?

Q What do you call a **playlist** on a **hiker's** music player?

A A trail mix.

Q Where does a **cruise ship** go when **it's** not feeling well?

A To the dock-tor.

A baseball team won 5–0 but not a single man ran around the bases. How is that possible?

All the men were married.

SURFER 1: Hey, why are you wearing a baseball mitt?

SURFER 2: Because you said we were going to catch some waves.

Did you know that within **one day** of being **born,** a baby **mountain goat,** or kid, can climb rocks and mountains with its mother?

You can tell the age of a mountain goat by counting the rings on its horns.

Q What do you get if you cross a creek and a river?

Wet feet.

A

TERRIBLE SAFARI ADVERTISEMENTS:

☐ Ever wanted to smell a rhino's breath?

☐ The world's first walking tour of Lion's Cove!

☐ Run with the wildebeests!

☐ Tour Leopard's Lair—the first 10 bandages are free!

Q

What do chickens do on Sunday afternoons?

They go on peck-nics.

A

SAY WHAT?

NAMES
Slipper and Slider

FAVORITE ACTIVITY
Skiing

FAVORITE FOOD
Snow cones

PET PEEVE
Wearing the same outfit as someone else

WADDLE WE DO TODAY?

I LOVE CHILLIN' WITH MY PEEPS.

While penguins are molting, or shedding their feathers, they can't go in the water to hunt. They have to fatten themselves up to prepare for fasting during these few weeks.

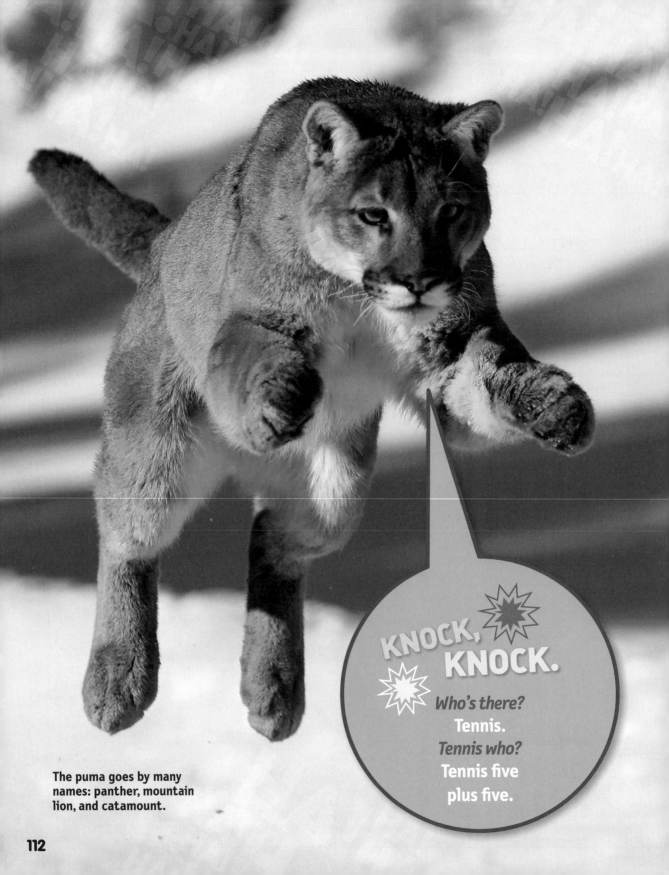

The puma goes by many names: panther, mountain lion, and catamount.

KNOCK, KNOCK.

Who's there?
Tennis.
Tennis who?
Tennis five plus five.

RIDDLE ✹ ME THIS

At what **school** do you have to **drop out** in order to graduate?

Skydiving school.

Q Why aren't artists good at sports?

A Every game ends in a draw.

Q Why shouldn't you play **football** with a **pig?**

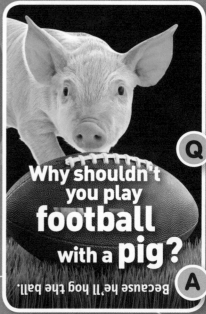

A Because he'll hog the ball.

Q Why did the teacher wear sunglasses on her school trip?

Because her students were so bright.

A

What **lights up** a stadium?

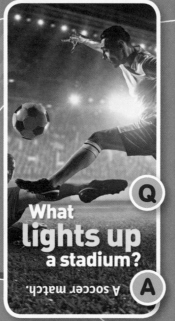

A A soccer match.

CUSTOMER: I'm leaving for my cruise, and I need to pick up my laundry.
DRY CLEANER: Okay, let me just see if I can find it.
CUSTOMER: Hurry! Hurry! I don't want to miss my boat.
DRY CLEANER: All right, all right, keep your shirt on.

Q What did the **sardine** call the **submarine tour?**

A can of people.

A

Q How did the **barber** win the **cross-country race?**

He took a shortcut.

A

Q Which baseball player pours the lemonade?

The pitcher.

A

113

Q Which **people travel the most?**

A Roam-ans.

MARATHON RUNNER: I'm here for my pre-race checkup, doc.
DOCTOR: Well, you seem to be in fantastic condition. Your pulse is like clockwork.
MARATHON RUNNER: That's because your finger is on my watch!

Q What do **birds** use when **skydiving?**

A Sparrow-chutes.

Q Why did the orange stop climbing halfway up the mountain?

A It ran out of juice.

Q What do you call the **slowest competitor** in a downhill **ski race?**

A A slope-poke.

Q Which is the **noisiest sport?**

A Racket-ball.

Q Why **didn't the girl take** the **bus home** from her **camping trip?**

A Because her mom would make her bring it back.

An elephant's ears release body heat to help keep it cool in hot temperatures.

Q What does the **winner** of a **marathon lose?**

A Her breath.

CARRIE: I'm learning to surf in my kitchen.
CHARLOTTE: Where?
CARRIE: On a micro-wave!

LOL ADVENTURE

In 2015, a woman set a **WORLD RECORD** for **fastest marathon run** while dressed as a **FAST-FOOD ITEM.**

Despite their funny appearance, **RODEO CLOWNS** are **trained bullfighters** whose primary job is **protecting** fallen riders from the **BULLS.**

Runners in an annual Seattle, U.S.A., **marathon** can **EAT CAKE** at aid stations and rest on **COUCHES** along the **running course.**

In the 1800s, **WATER POLO** was played on **floating barrels** that looked like **HORSES.**

CHAPTER 5

Wacky World

HA!HA!HA!HA!
HA!HA!
HA!HA!
HA!HA!

GARRY:
What channel are the Japanese origami championships on?
ROBERTO:
You can only watch it on paper-view.

Q Where do Canadian sheep come from?

A Manito-baa.

HAS ANYONE SEEN MY MUMMY?

Q What kind of pastry comes from Britain?

An English muffin. **A**

TONGUE TWISTER!

Say this fast three times:

Norwegian boys need noisy, annoying toys.

Did you know that the **Pyramid** of **Khufu** at **Giza** is the largest **Egyptian pyramid?**

It's estimated to be made up of about 2.4 million stone blocks weighing 2.5 tons (2.3 t) each.

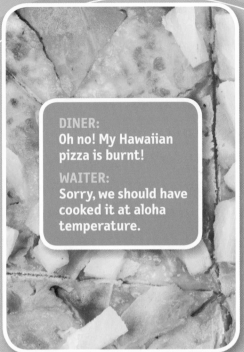

DINER:
Oh no! My Hawaiian pizza is burnt!

WAITER:
Sorry, we should have cooked it at aloha temperature.

RIDDLE ME THIS

What travels around the world, but never leaves its corner?

A stamp.

Q

What can you find in the middle of the ocean?

The letter e.

A

Q

What do Canadians score on their tests?

Ehs. **A**

Q Which country has the most birds?

A Portu-gull.

Q Which city receives the most deliveries?

A Parcel-ona.

JOSH: Where do you want to go on vacation?
DYLAN: I'd like to go to Holland, wooden shoe?

Q Why don't seals go on vacation in the United Kingdom?

A Because they're afraid of Wales.

Q What keeps lions from leaving the savanna?

A The ele-fence.

Q What do you call a rabbit in a kilt?

A Hop Scotch.

Q What did Tennessee?

A The same thing Arkansas.

THE WORST PART ABOUT TRAVEL IS PACKING.

RIDDLE ✹ ✹ ME THIS

What has a **mouth** but **can't talk**, a **head** but **can't think**, a **bed** but **doesn't sleep**, and can **run** but **never walk**?

A river.

122

KNOCK, KNOCK.

Who's there?
Iraq.
Iraq who?
Iraq-ed my brain to think of something fun to do.

Churchill, in Manitoba, Canada, is the polar bear capital of the world. The bears pass through the city during their migration.

KNOCK, KNOCK.

Who's there?
Iran.
Iran who?
Iran all the way here.

Blue eyes are common in just a few dog breeds, such as Siberian huskies and Australian shepherds.

Q Where do angry chickens come from?

A Mad-egg-ascar.

Q What's the **craziest** way **to travel?**

A By loco-motive.

Q Why does the Mississippi River see so well?

A Because it has four i's.

Q What is the Amazon rain forest's favorite month?

A Sep-timber.

Q Where in the United States do you find the funkiest dancers?

A San Fran-disco.

JULIA: Jamaica dinner yet? I'm hungry.
EWAN: Not yet, but Alaska everyone what they want to eat.

TONGUE TWISTER!

Say this fast three times:

The gracious Greek geek agreed.

I KNEW WE SHOULD HAVE GOTTEN HERE EARLY. TOURISTS FLOCK TO THIS PLACE.

Q Which **country eats** the **most soup?**

A Bowl-ivia.

NAMES Latitude and Longitude

FAVORITE ACTIVITY Leisurely Sunday drives

FAVORITE TOY GPS

PET PEEVE Speeding tickets

I HAVE A FEAR OF SPEED BUMPS, BUT I'M SLOWLY GETTING OVER IT.

WE'RE GOING ON A THREE-WEEK VACATION ... WE'RE GOING TO WALK TO THE OTHER SIDE OF THIS FOREST.

THIS VACATION IS GOING TO BE SLOTHSOME!

I LOVE TRAVELING SLOW MUCH!

Sloths live in tropical climates in Central and South America.

Q Which **country** has the **most marathons?**

A Iran.

TEACHER: Why didn't you study for your geography test?

ASTRONAUT: My dad says the world is changing every day so I thought I'd wait until it stops.

LAUGHABLE LIST

SIGNS YOU ARE DRIVING THROUGH A DESERT ON YOUR ROAD TRIP:

☐ You eat hot wings to cool your mouth off.

☐ When the temperature drops below 98°F (37°C), you put on a sweater.

☐ Cows are giving evaporated milk.

☐ The cacti are sitting in the shade.

☐ Vultures are taking the day off.

ANTHONY: Where were you born?
PRIYA: In India.
ANTHONY: Which part?
PRIYA: All of me!

Did you know that **Machu Picchu's** construction is still a **mystery?**

It's not known how the massive stone blocks were moved up the steep terrain and through thick jungles.

Q Which state is the loudest?

A Illi-noise.

At **night** they come without being called. In the **morning** they are **lost** without being stolen. **What are they?**

Stars.

Q

Why is the River Thames so rich?

A Because it has two banks.

MACHU PICCHU PHOTOBOMB!

Q

Which country never stays still?

Romania.

A

129

A MOTHER WAS WALKING BY HER DAUGHTER'S ROOM one night and saw her daughter staring out the window. "What are you doing, sweetie?" the mother asked.

"I'm making a wish on that shooting star," the girl replied.

"Oh, that's nice. What are you wishing for?" her mother asked.

"I'm wishing that the capital of the United States is Albany," the girl answered.

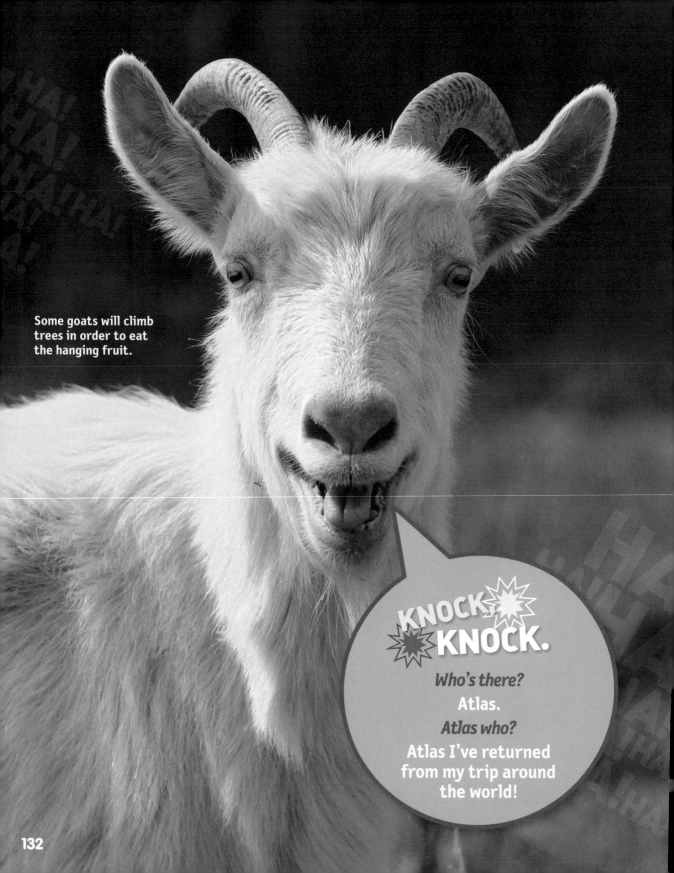

Some goats will climb trees in order to eat the hanging fruit.

KNOCK KNOCK.

Who's there?
Atlas.
Atlas who?
Atlas I've returned from my trip around the world!

Say this fast three times:

Helga is hoping to hop to Tahiti.

Q Which U.S. city has the most chickens?

A Chick-ago.

Q What did the Kinderdijk windmills say to the visiting movie star?

A "I'm your biggest fan!"

Q Which is the **spiciest country?**

A Chile.

Q Who is a penguin's favorite relative?

A Aunt Arctica.

Q What type of planes do snakes travel on?

A Boeing constrictors.

Q

Why should you never play hide-and-seek with Mount Everest?

A Because it always peaks.

TEACHER: Where is the English Channel?
MARY: It must be far away because my TV doesn't pick it up.

Q Why did the **Louvre pyramid** go to **the doctor?**

A Because it had window panes.

133

A group of tortoises is called a creep.

KNOCK, KNOCK.

Who's there?

Juneau.

Juneau who?

Juneau how cold Alaska is?

Q What is **Mount Rushmore's** favorite **music**?

A Rock-and-roll.

Q Which **state has terrible allergies?**

A Mass-achoo-setts.

Q How do you open the **Great Lakes?**

A With the Florida Keys.

Q What is Mount Etna's favorite meal?

A Magma-roni and cheese.

SON: Where do bees come from?
MOTHER: Sting-apore and Bee-livia.

Q Where do you find an **ocean** without **water?**

A On a map.

Q Where do you take your **unpaid electric bill?**

A I-owe-a.

Q What do you call an Australian boomerang that doesn't come back after you throw it?

A A stick.

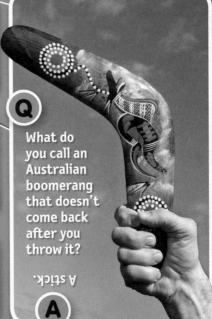

Q Which **state** has the **cleanest clothes?**

A Wash-ington.

Q How do Notre-Dame Cathedral's statues cure their sore throats?

A By gargoyling.

TEACHER: Can anyone tell me where elephants are found?

STUDENT: How does anyone lose an elephant?!

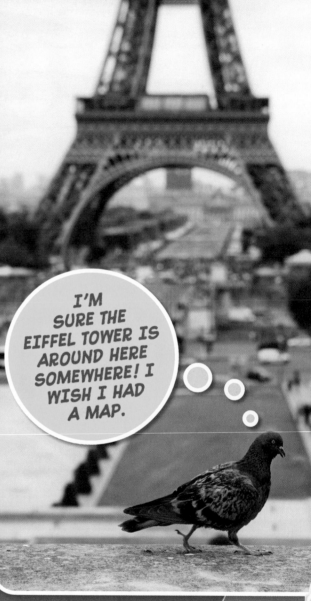

I'M SURE THE EIFFEL TOWER IS AROUND HERE SOMEWHERE! I WISH I HAD A MAP.

Q Why doesn't anyone want to be **friends** with **Big Ben?**

A Because all it does it tock, tock, tock.

Q Why can't you **trust the Atlantic Ocean?**

A Because there is something fishy about it.

Did you know that some **pigeons** were **war heroes?** Messenger pigeons carried notes and intelligence from behind enemy lines during **World War I** and **World War II.**

Pigeons can be found on every continent except Antarctica.

TRAVELER 1: How was your trip?
TRAVELER 2: Great! I got Hungary in Italy, so I ate some Turkey. How was your trip?
TRAVELER 1: Not so good, I slipped on Greece and got bitten by Wales.

Q

How did Christopher Columbus's men sleep on their ships?

A

With their eyes closed.

Q

Why can't you make a reservation at the Library of Congress?

Because it's completely booked.

A

Q

What state has the most horses?

Neigh-braska.

A

SAY WHAT?

NAME
Globe Trotter

FAVORITE ACTIVITY
Horsing around

FAVORITE DANCE
The Neigh Neigh

PET PEEVE
Bad weather ...
especially reins

QUIT STALLING, IT'S TIME TO LEAVE!

KNOCK, KNOCK.
Who's there?
Neigh.
Neigh who?
I just met your neighbors.

WE DON'T WANT TO MISS THE MANE EVENT.

Horses sleep standing up. They "lock" their legs to stop themselves from collapsing while asleep.

138

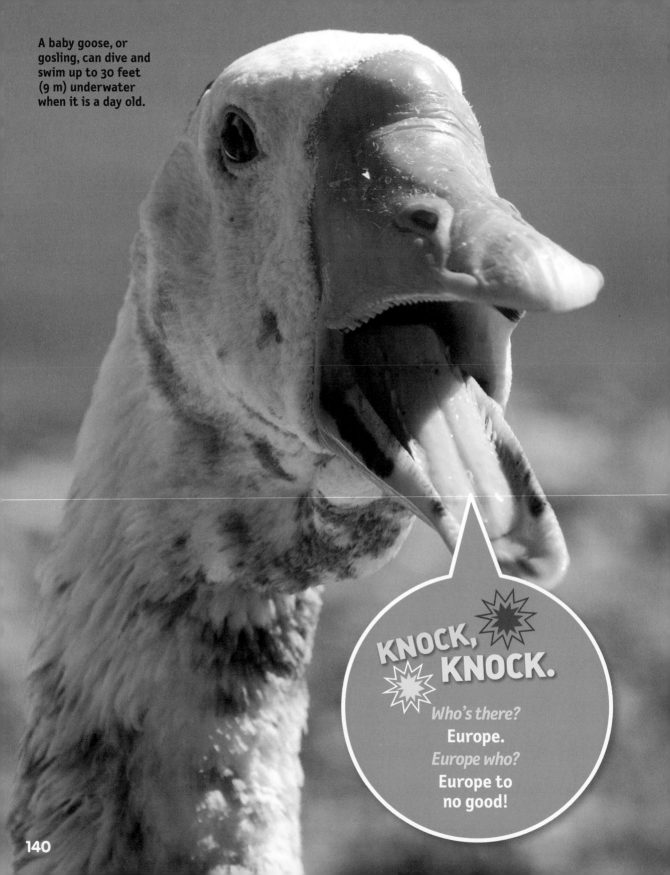

A baby goose, or gosling, can dive and swim up to 30 feet (9 m) underwater when it is a day old.

KNOCK, KNOCK.

Who's there?
Europe.
Europe who?
Europe to no good!

They **run fast** but can't stand. You **ride them** like **horses** but they don't eat grass. You can **find** them all over the world. What are they?

Bicycles.

LOCKSMITH 1:
Where do you want to go on vacation?
LOCKSMITH 2:
To the Florida Keys.

Q What do you get if you cross **Godzilla** and a **kangaroo?**

Great big holes all over Australia.

A

Q What kind of hair does the **Atlantic Ocean** have?

Wavy.

A

Q What is the cheapest way to travel?

By sale-boat.

A **A**

Q Why did the sailors carry a bar of soap with them?

In case they got shipwrecked, they could wash themselves up on shore.

A

SOAP

Q Where do fish keep their money?

In the riverbank.

A

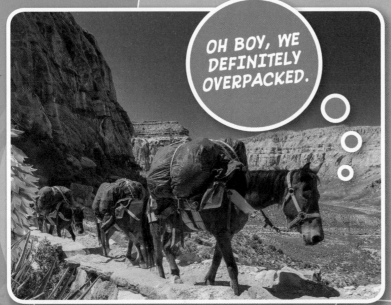

OH BOY, WE DEFINITELY OVERPACKED.

IAN: Can a bunny hop higher than the Empire State Building?
BEN: Yes, the Empire State Building can't hop.

Koalas rarely drink water. They get most of the moisture they need from eating eucalyptus leaves.

KNOCK, KNOCK.

Who's there?
Havana.
Havana who?
Havana great time in Cuba!

Q Which landmark has the best manners?

A The Leaning Tower of Please-a.

Q What do you call a type of Mexican food served at the North Pole?

A Brrr-itos.

Q Which little rivers run into the Nile?

A Juve-niles.

Q Which rock group has four men that don't sing?

A Mount Rushmore.

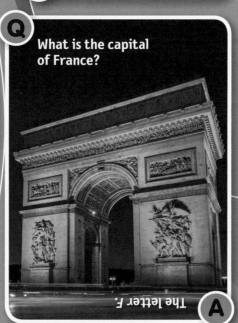

Q What is the capital of France?

A The letter F.

Q What do you get if you cross a farm animal and a mapmaker?

A A cow-tographer.

Q Which state is the hardest to find?

A Dela-where?

Q Why was the vacationing doctor so angry?

A He had no patients.

TEACHER: Jack, point to where America is on the map.
JACK: Right there.
TEACHER: That's correct. Nina, who discovered America?
NINA: Jack did.

LOL WORLD

...st annual **Laughing** ...pionships **were held** ...Quebec, Canada, **in 2001.** ...Contests included: **Best Maniacal Laugh and Most Contagious Belly Laugh.**

In Japan, **it's considered** impolite **to SHOW YOUR TEETH while** laughing.

...nd, **people text** ..."5" ...of ..."a" ...to ...g

MY OPTOMETRIST USES AN EYE-PHONE.

5555

A laughter epidemic broke out in a girls' school **and spread to** **1,000 PEOPLE in Tanzania, Africa, in 1962.**

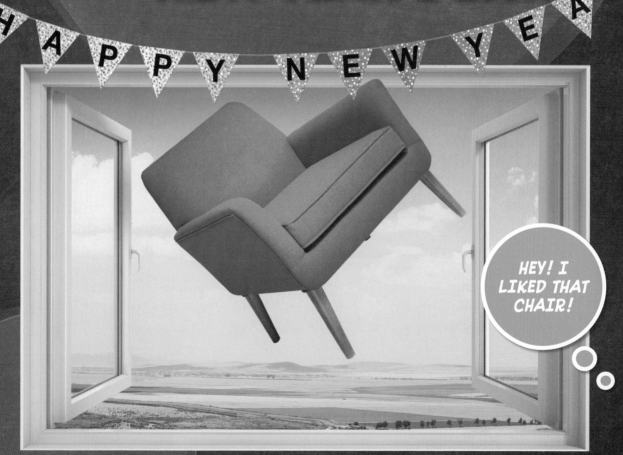

IN SOME PARTS OF SOUTH AFRICA, PEOPLE **THROW FURNITURE OUT THE WINDOW** TO CELEBRATE NEW YEAR'S DAY.

HAPPY NEW YEAR

HEY! I LIKED THAT CHAIR!

CHAPTER 6

Animal Antics

Ants can carry 50 times their own body weight. That would be like you lifting a car!

147

LAUGHABLE LIST

NEW DOG BREEDS:

☐ Collie + Lhasa apso = Collapso: folds up to fit into small doghouses

☐ German shepherd + cocker spaniel = Shocker: a dog that's always surprising you

☐ Collie + malamute = Comute: you have to travel a long way to find one

☐ Afghan + Labrador retriever = Afghan retriever: brings you a blanket

☐ Shar-pei + German pointer = Sharp point: be careful when petting this one

SANJIDA: Oh no! 500 hares have escaped from the zoo!
PRIYA: Don't worry, the police are combing the area.
SANJIDA: I hope every bunny gets home safe.

RIDDLE ✸ ME THIS

What grows up while growing down?

·ǝsooƃ ∀

I FIND THESE JOKES A-MOOSE-ING!

Q Why did the pig drop out of the marathon?

8725 MARATHON

·ƃuᴉɹʇsɯɐɥ ɐ pǝllnd ʇᴉ ǝsnɐɔǝB **A**

Q What do you call a member of the weasel family that likes to knit?

A A wool-ver-ine.

What do you call **baby owls** that get **stuck** in the rain?

Q

A Moist owlets.

Did you know that a **moose's antlers** can grow to be **six feet (1.8 m) wide** and weigh up to 70 pounds (32 kg)?

Adult moose shed their antlers every winter.

TONGUE TWISTER!

Say this fast three times:

Three-toed tree toad.

Q **Why was the sheep itchy?**

A It had fleece.

COW 1: Hey, who's the new calf?
COW 2: I don't know, I've never seen herbivore.

149

What do you call a COW that doesn't give milk?

A: An udder failure.

What sits when it stands, and jumps when it walks?

A: A kangaroo.

Say this fast three times:

A skunk thunk the stump stunk.

Q: **Where do lambs share their videos?**

A: On ewe-tube.

Q: **Why are there different blood types?**

A: So mosquitoes can enjoy different flavors.

Q: **What do you get if you cross a flower and a zoo animal?**

A: A rhinoce-rose.

Q: What do you get if you cross a snake and a piece of fruit?

A: A banana-conda.

Q: Why do cows wear bells around their neck?

A: Because their horns don't work.

ZOO KEEPER 1: Why did you measure this snake in inches?
ZOO KEEPER 2: Because they don't have feet.

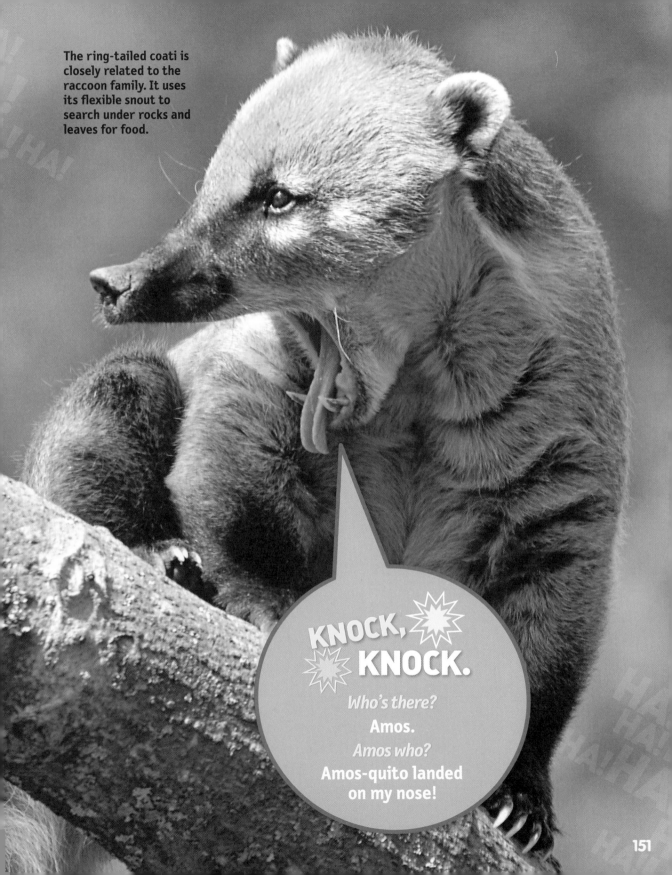

The ring-tailed coati is closely related to the raccoon family. It uses its flexible snout to search under rocks and leaves for food.

KNOCK, KNOCK.

Who's there?

Amos.

Amos who?

Amos-quito landed on my nose!

151

Gulls are able to drink saltwater. They have "salt glands" that filter the salt and trickle the excess out through their nostrils.

KNOCK, KNOCK.

Who's there?
Quack.
Quack who?
Quack another bad joke and I'm leaving.

Q Why did the chicken go to the movies?

A For hen-tertainment.

Q What is a marsupial's favorite soft drink?

A Coca-Koala.

MOM COW: It's time for bed!
CALF: Do I calf to go?
MOM COW: Yes, it's pasture bedtime.

RIDDLE ☀ ☀ ME THIS

A **horse** is tied to a **10-foot (3-m) rope** and there is a bale of hay **20 feet (6 m)** away from him but the horse can still eat from it. **How is that possible?**

The other end of the rope isn't tied to anything.

Q Why did the pig give his girlfriend a box of chocolates?

A Because it was Valen-swine's Day.

Q Why do snails need their shells to race?

A Without them, they are sluggish.

Q What does a penguin eat at a barbecue?

A An iceberg-er.

KEEP LOOKING, I KNOW WE PARKED THE CAR AROUND HERE SOMEWHERE.

154

SPOTS ARE SO LAST SEASON.

A zebra's teeth will grow for its entire life. Zebras graze and chew on tough grasses constantly, which wears their teeth down.

KNOCK, KNOCK.

Who's there?

Rhino.

Rhino who?

Rhino every knock-knock joke there is.

Q

Where do frozen chickens live?

A In egg-loos.

Q

What do you call an owl that does magic tricks?

A Hoo-dini.

EXCUSE ME, SIR ... PARDON ME, MA'AM ... JUST TRYING TO REACH MY SEAT ON THE END.

YOUR FOOT IS IN MY EYE!

Q

What do you call a sneaky pig?

A Cunningham.

Q What sort of shoes do frogs wear to the beach?

A Open-toed sandals.

Did you know that **tree frogs** have **disc-shaped toes** that give its feet more suction and a better grip?

They live in forests and jungles in warm regions around the world.

RIDDLE ME THIS

If a **rooster** laid a **brown egg** and a **white egg,** what color **chicks** would hatch?

None, roosters don't lay eggs.

NICO: Oh no! My seahorse ran away!
MACEO: Actually, it was more of a scallop.

SQUIRREL 1: You walnut guess what happened! I forget where I buried the cashews!
SQUIRREL 2: You're nuttin' but trouble.

A WOMAN WAS DRIVING AND SAW A TRUCK BROKEN DOWN ON THE SIDE OF THE ROAD. The woman pulled over and offered some help to the driver.

The truck driver said, "That would be great! Can you please take the 10 lions I have in the back of my truck to the zoo while I fix my tire? I'll give you $50."

The woman agreed. She took the money and the lions and drove away.

Two hours later, the truck driver spotted the woman and the lions walking out of a theater. He pulled over and yelled, "What are you doing? You were supposed to take those lions to the zoo!"

The woman answered, "I did, but we had some money left over so we went to the movies!"

KNOCK, KNOCK.

Who's there?

Herring.

Herring who?

Herring some awful
knock-knock jokes.

Lionfish have up to 18
venomous spines which are
used only for self-defense.

TONGUE TWISTER!

Say this fast three times:

Bamboo baboon.

FARMER 1: Why does this chicken coop only have two doors?

FARMER 2: Because if it had four it would be a sedan.

Q Why do elephants have trunks?

A Because they don't have pockets to put their stuff in.

Q Where do cows go for lunch?

A The calf-eteria.

Q Why did the farmer cross the road?

A To get his chicken back.

Q Where do goats get their medicine?

A From the farm-acy.

Q Where does a **bull** keep his **important papers?**

A In his beef-case.

Q What do you call an **angry grizzly** bear?

A Furry-ous.

OUR SELFIE GAME IS ON POINT.

161

KNOCK, KNOCK.

Who's there?

Fleas.

Fleas who?

Fleas a jolly good fellow.

I'M JUST GOING TO HAVE A QUICK SNACK, AND THEN IT'S OFF TO SCHOOL.

When confronted by a predator, meerkats will group together, arch their backs, and hiss to try to trick the attacker into thinking they are one large, fierce animal.

Q What do you get if you cross a **shark** and a **cow?**

A I don't know, but I wouldn't try to milk it!

Q What do you call a **lazy marsupial?**

A A pouch potato.

Q What do you call a **gossipy monkey?**

A A blab-oon.

Q Which **birds** always **stick together?**

A Vel-crows.

Q What do you get if you cross an elephant and a skin doctor?

A A pachyderm-atologist.

BABY CAMEL: Dad, can I have another glass of water?
FATHER CAMEL: Another one? That's the second glass this month!

163

Q
What do you call
two squids
that look **exactly** alike?

Q
Which
animal
complains
the most?

A A whine-oceros.

BEAR: I'll have a
hamburger and ... fries.
WAITER: Okay, but why
the big pause?
BEAR: I was
born with
them!

LOOK! NO
CAVITIES!

Q
What do you get if you squeeze
an alpaca and a citrus fruit at
the same time?

A Llama-nade.

Q
How do
grizzlies
keep their
dens **cool** in
the summer?

With bear-conditioning.

A

Q

What do **mallards** like to watch on **TV?**

A Duck-umentaries.

A I-tentacle twins.

Did you know that the **closest relatives** to the **hippo** are **cetaceans** such as whales and dolphins?

A hippo's ears and nostrils fold shut to keep water out while swimming.

Q What **prizes** are awarded at the **pig** Olympics?

A Pork medallions.

Q

What do chimpanzees wear when they barbecue?

A Ape-rons.

FELIX: Why does your mother keep saying "Cluck, cluck, cluck"?
STEVE: She thinks she's a chicken.
FELIX: So why don't you stop her?
STEVE: Because we ran out of eggs.

165

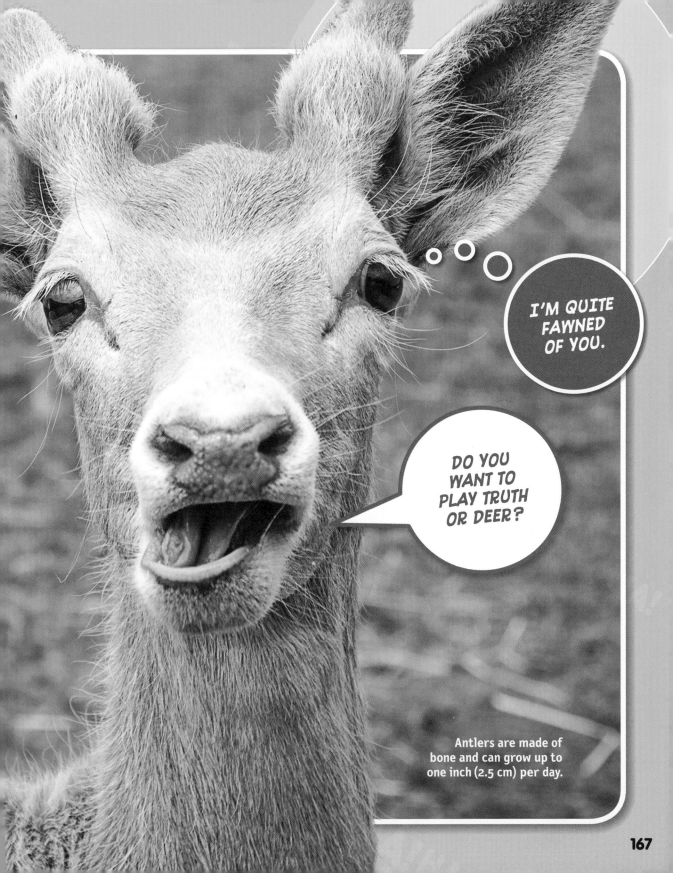

Antlers are made of
bone and can grow up to
one inch (2.5 cm) per day.

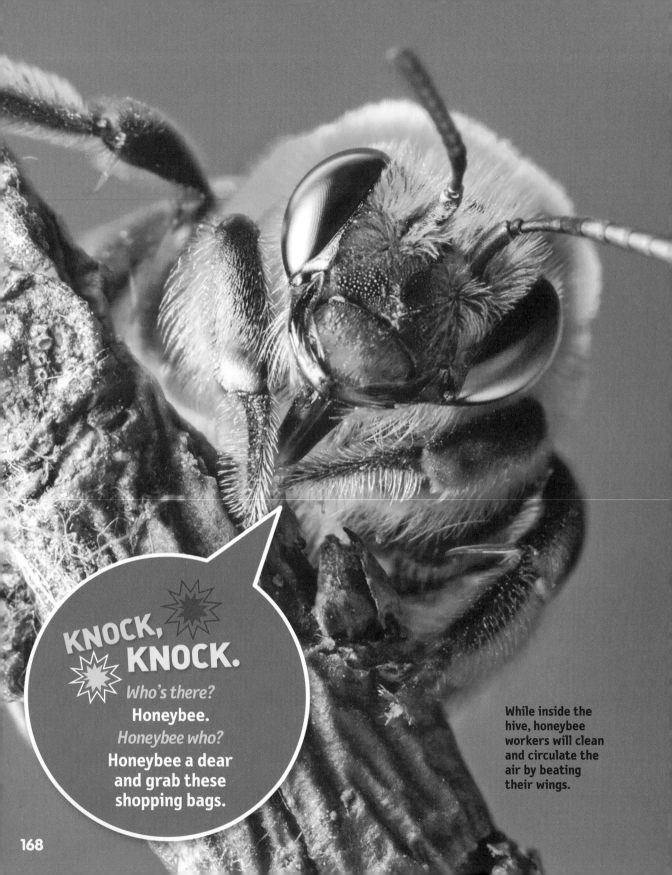

KNOCK, KNOCK.

Who's there?
Honeybee.
Honeybee who?
Honeybee a dear and grab these shopping bags.

While inside the hive, honeybee workers will clean and circulate the air by beating their wings.

Q What do you call a group of pigs running toward you?

A A ham-pede.

Q What do cats use to mix pancake batter?

A Their own whiskers.

Q What do you call a **thieving alligator?**

A A crook-odile.

SHOPPER:
I'd like 30 bags of birdseed, please.
PET STORE OWNER:
Wow! How many birds do you have?
SHOPPER:
None, I'd like to grow some.

Q What side of a cheetah has the most spots?

A The outside.

Q Why did the **pig** stop **sunbathing?**

A Because he was bacon in the heat.

Q What kind of **coffee** do **COWS** drink?

Bessie

A De-calf-inated.

Q Why can't an emu fly?

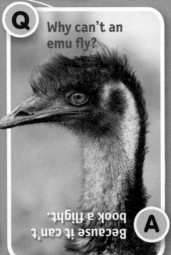

A Because it can't book a flight.

Q What time do **ducks** get out of bed?

A At the quack of dawn.

169

KNOCK, KNOCK.

Who's there?
Gorilla.
Gorilla who?
I'd love a gorilla cheese sandwich.

Though a mandrill's teeth can look scary, baring them is a friendly gesture among other mandrills.

Q What kind of big cats join you for breakfast?
A Sausage lynx.

Q What do you call a cranky bee?
A A grumble-bee.

LIBRARIAN: Can I help you find anything?
OWL: Can you point me to the mystery section? I love to read hoot-dunits.

Q Which sea creatures hang out at the gym?
A Mussels.

Q What kind of key opens a banana?
A A monkey.

Q Why didn't anyone speak to the pig at the costume party?
A Because everyone thought it was a boar.

Q What kind of fruit do gorillas eat?
A Ape-ricots.

Q Why do centipedes have 100 legs?
A So they can walk.

Q What do you call a penguin in the jungle?
A Lost.

DUCK: Hello, I'd like to buy some lipstick.
SALESPERSON: Sure thing, are you paying with cash or should I put it on your bill?

LOL ANIMALS

Mosquitoes prefer to **BITE** people with **SMELLY** feet.

COCKROACHES get gassy from eating cucumbers.

One species of **turtle** can breathe through its **REAR END**.

One species of **CICADA** makes a sound similar to **human LAUGHTER.**

SPOTTED HYENAS ARE OFTEN CALLED **LAUGHING HYENAS** BECAUSE OF THE **LOUD,** HIGH-PITCHED **GIGGLING** SOUND THEY MAKE.

I'VE GOT A SERIOUS CASE OF THE GIGGLES!

173

Merry Myths & Funny Fables

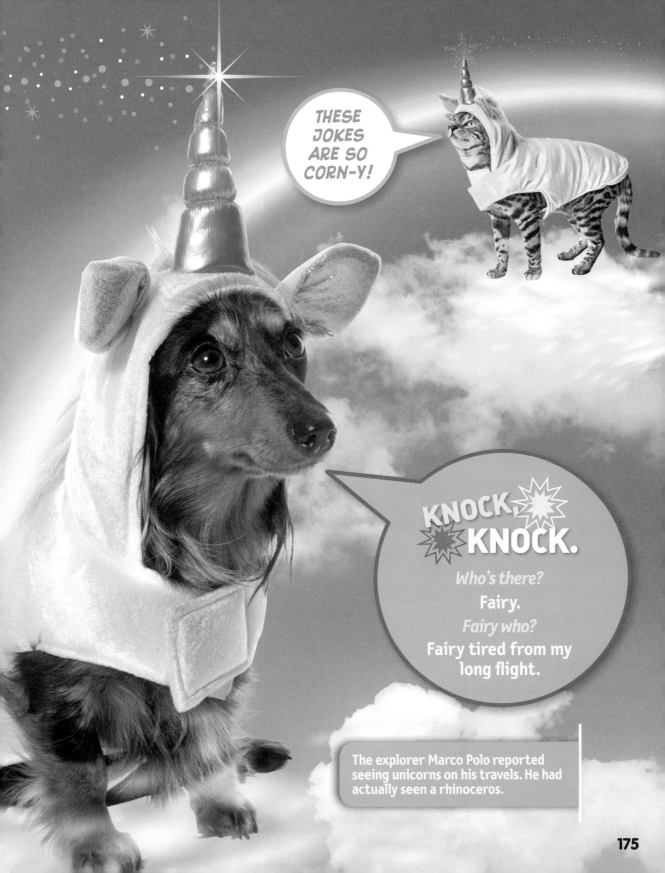

175

Q What do you get if you cross a **fairy tale** and a **ghost story?**

A Ghoul-dilocks and the Three Bears.

BRAD:
Did you see the guy at the costume party dressed as half man, half horse?

GABRIEL:
Yes, he certainly was the centaur of attention.

Did you know that the **unicorn** is **Scotland's national animal?**

The unicorn appears in chains on the country's coat of arms to suggest that Scottish kings were strong enough to tame the unicorn.

WHAT DO I WEAR TO WORK? MY UNI-FORM OF COURSE!

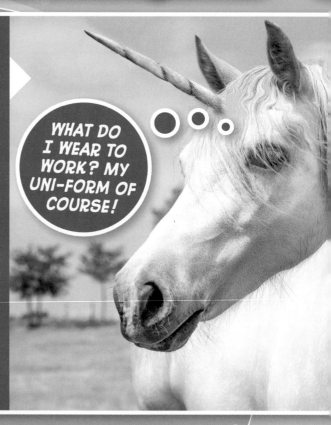

Q Why do you **never** see **dragons** out during the day?

A Because they usually hunt knights.

What's the difference between a goblin and a head of lettuce?

A

One is a funny beast and the other is a bunny feast.

MERMAN: I've heard some people don't trust the ocean.
MERWOMAN: Really? Why is that?
MERMAN: They think there's something fishy about it.

LAUGHABLE LIST

LESSER KNOWN GREEK GODS:

- ☐ Typos—god of proofreaders
- ☐ Mintees—god of fresh breath
- ☐ Spectaclees—god of improved eyesight
- ☐ Cheapos—god of saving money
- ☐ Tartemis—god of tasty pastries
- ☐ Lieclops—god of mistruths

Q What does a **Greek goddess** do to pamper herself?

She makes a Hera-pointment.

A

Q

Why did Captain Hook cross the road?

A To get to the second-hand shop.

Q

What was it like planning **Goliath's funeral?**

A A giant undertaking.

Q

What do you call someone with a callus on one foot?

A A uni-corn.

Q

Why was **Zeus so angry?**

A Someone stole his thunder.

Q

What did **Kraken** eat for **lunch?**

A Fish and ships.

MARIE: Do you know what's in Aladdin's lamp?
MARCUS: It wouldn't take a genie-ous to find out.

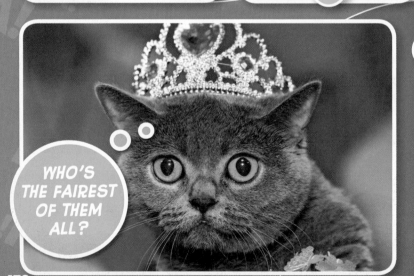

WHO'S THE FAIREST OF THEM ALL?

Q

What do you get when you cross an archer and a gift-wrapper?

A Ribbon Hood.

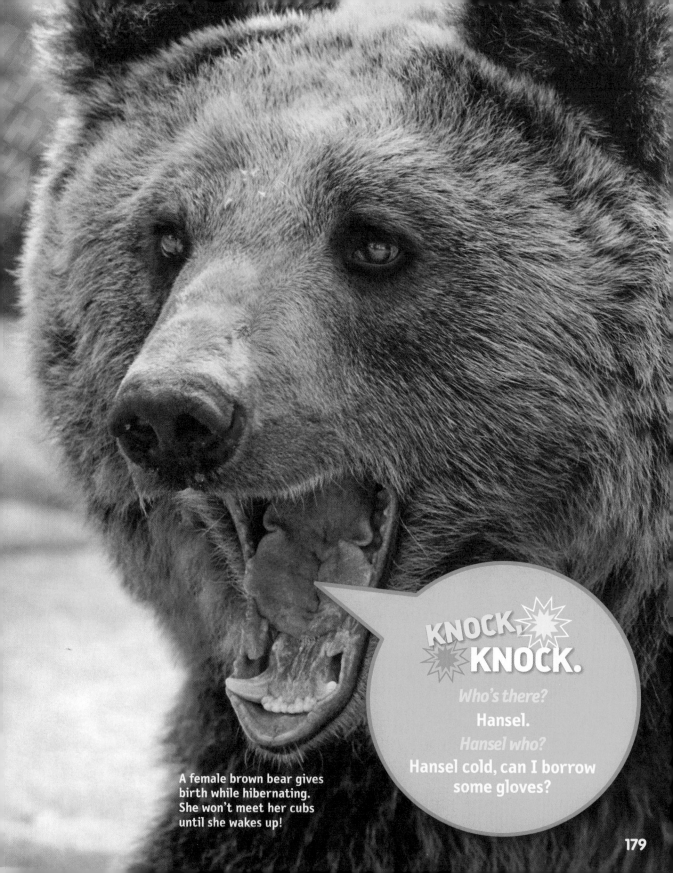

A female brown bear gives birth while hibernating. She won't meet her cubs until she wakes up!

KNOCK, KNOCK.
Who's there?
Hansel.
Hansel who?
Hansel cold, can I borrow some gloves?

179

Hippos mainly eat at night and can consume up to 150 pounds (68 kg) of grass.

KNOCK, KNOCK.

Who's there?
Gretel.
Gretel who?
We Gretel long great with each other!

Q What do you call the story of "The Three Little Pigs"?

A A pigtail.

Q Why would **Snow White** make a great judge?

A Because she's the fairest in the land.

Why did Cinderella get kicked off the baseball team?

Q

A She kept running away from the ball.

Q What do dragons put in their soup?

A Firecrackers.

Q What do you call a fairy that hasn't bathed?

A Stinker-bell.

RIDDLE ✹ ME THIS

A **fairy** lives in a **one-story house** with a **blue** couch, **blue** walls, and **blue** carpets. **What color are her stairs?**

There are no stairs in a one-story house.

HUMPTY DUMPTY: Why are all the king's men so short?
KING: They're all 12 inches tall.
HUMPTY DUMPTY: Does that mean they're foot soldiers?

THIS DOESN'T SEEM AS REGAL AS THE CROWN I HAD WHEN I WAS A HUMAN PRINCE.

Q Why was Cinderella so bad at sports?

A Because she had a pumpkin for a coach.

NAME **Thor**

FAVORITE ACTIVITY
Home renovations

FAVORITE TOY
Enchanted hammer

PET PEEVE
Hitting my thumb

ODIN SENT SECRET MESSAGES BY NORSE CODE.

I'M A-FREYA-D OF SCARY MYTHS.

A hammerhead shark's head is the perfect shape for trapping stingrays and pinning them to the seafloor before eating them.

KNOCK, KNOCK.

Who's there?

Euripides.

Euripides who?

Euripides jeans, I'm going to be mad.

OPTICIAN: Have your eyes ever been checked before?
DRAGON: No, they've always been red.

Q How did Jack figure out how many beans to sell his cow for?

A With a cow-culator.

KNOCK, KNOCK? ANYBODY GNOME?

Q What do you get when you cross a **mythical creature** and a **stiletto heel?**

A A shoe-nicorn.

Q Why did Miss Muffet have GPS on her tuffet?

A To keep from losing her whey.

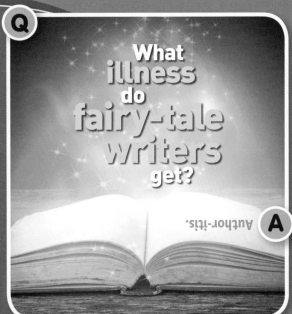

Q What illness do fairy-tale writers get?

A Author-itis.

Did you know that **NASA** sent **ladybugs** and **aphids** into space to see how long the aphids could escape from the ladybugs in **zero gravity?**

Ladybugs are believed to be good luck in many cultures.

RIDDLE ✷ ME THIS ✷

The **more** that it **appeared,** the **less** Zeus could see. **What was it?**

Darkness.

JACK'S MOTHER:
Why is there always a conversation going on in the garden?
JACK'S FATHER:
Because Jack and his beans talk.

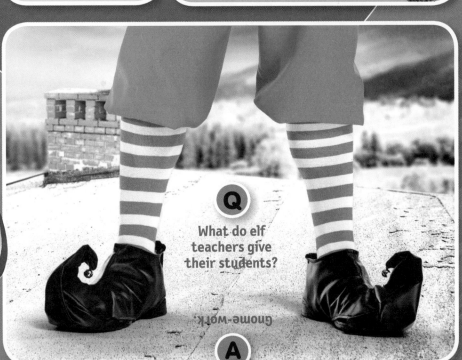

Q What do elf teachers give their students?

A Gnome-work.

THE THREE LITTLE PIGS **WENT OUT FOR DINNER.** When the waiter arrived to take their order, the first pig ordered a coffee, the second pig ordered a tea, and the third pig ordered water.

When the waiter came by again, the first pig ordered soup, the second pig ordered a sandwich, but the third pig ordered another glass of water.

When the waiter returned to take their dessert order, the first pig ordered pie, the second pig ordered cake, and the third pig ordered yet another glass of water.

"Excuse me," the waiter said to the third pig, "why have you ordered nothing but water all evening?"

The third pig replied, "Well one of us has to wee, wee, wee, all the way home!"

Despite their name, red pandas are actually close relatives of the raccoon.

KNOCK, KNOCK.

Who's there?

Althea.

Althea who?

Althea later, alligator!

Q What did **Cinderella** say when the **photos** she ordered didn't **show up?**

A "Someday my prints will come."

Q What did Little **Red Riding Hood** say when she saw the wolf wearing sunglasses?

A Nothing. She didn't recognize him.

Q Why was the mermaid riding a seahorse?

A Because she was playing water polo.

ALADDIN: I wish for a fur coat.
GENIE: What fur?
ALADDIN: To keep me warm, that's what fur!

Q What do you get if you cross **Tinkerbell** and a **peacock?**

A A lovely fairy tail.

Q Why did the Ugly Duckling's parents fly south for the winter?

A Because it was too far to walk.

Q Why did **Rapunzel** go to so many **parties?**

A Because she liked to let her hair down.

Q How did Robin Hood tie his shoelaces?

A With a long bow.

Q What do **unicorns call their fathers?**

A Pop-corns.

189

KNOCK, KNOCK.

Who's there?

Keith.

Keith who?

If I Keith a frog, will it turn into a prince?

Humboldt penguins can rocket through the water at speeds of 30 miles an hour (48 km/h).

Q What's brown, furry, and has 12 paws?

A The Three Bears.

TONGUE TWISTER!

Say this fast three times:

Which wicked witches wear watches?

Q Where do ogres dance?

A At the odd ball.

Q What did the sea monster say to the comedian?

A You're Kraken me up!

GREEK GOD 1: Have you seen any movies about Greek mythology?
GREEK GOD 2: No, are they any good?
GREEK GOD 1: Oh yes! You really Odyssey them.

Q What's gray, wears glass slippers, and weighs more than a car?

A Cinderella-phant.

Q What do elves learn in school?

A The elf-abet.

Q Why didn't Goldilocks eat all of her porridge?

A Because it was un-bear-able.

Q Why is Peter Pan always flying?

A Because he Neverlands.

191

Q What kind of **pet** did **Aladdin** have?

A A flying car-pet.

I AM PUG-SEIDON! DOG OF THE SEA! THAT'S WHY MY HELMET IS MADE OF WATERMELON.

LAUGHABLE LIST

THE OTHER SEVEN DWARFS:

☐ Gassy
☐ Blotchy
☐ Stinky
☐ Wheezy
☐ Twitchy
☐ Lazy
☐ Bill

Q What does Tom Thumb drink?

A Condensed milk.

CHICKEN LITTLE:
It's raining! Our picnic will be ruined!
CHICKEN LITTLE'S MOM:
I don't mind a little fowl weather.

GOLDILOCKS:
I bought the *worst* thesaurus yesterday.
BABY BEAR:
Really?
GOLDILOCKS:
Oh yes ... not only is it terrible, it's terrible.

Did you know that **Poseidon** is the **Greek god** of the sea and the brother of Zeus?

He is usually shown with a three-pronged spear called a trident.

Q

Why won't the Big Bad Wolf ever find Little Red Riding Hood's granny again?

A Because she's going to be well grandma-flaged.

Q

On which side of the house did Jack grow his beanstalk?

A The outside.

Q

What kind of jokes does a unicorn tell?

A Corny ones.

DRAGON 1:
I just ate a knight in metal armor.
DRAGON 2:
Oh, I love those. They're crunchy on the outside and chewy on the inside.
DRAGON 1:
I didn't like it. I'm not a fan of canned food.

NAME
Prince Charming

FAVORITE ACTIVITY
Styling my hare

FAVORITE DANCE
The Bunny Hop

PET PEEVE
Dust bunnies under the bed

LITTLE RUDE RIDING HOOD NEVER VISITED HER GRANNY.

WHAT IS THE BIG BAD WOLF'S FAVORITE FRUIT? THE THREE LITTLE FIGS.

Rabbits come in all sizes. Some weigh less than a pound (0.5 kg) while other breeds can weigh up to 13 pounds (5.9 kg).

RAPUNZEL DIDN'T WANT LONG HAIR, BUT EVENTUALLY IT GREW ON HER.

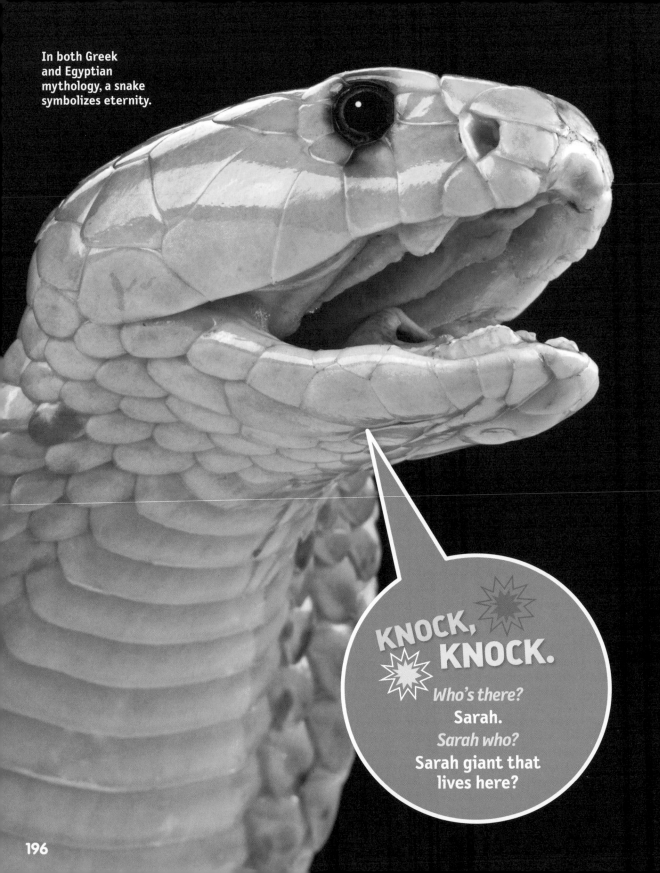

In both Greek and Egyptian mythology, a snake symbolizes eternity.

Q Why did Aladdin's lamp hum?

A Because the genie didn't know the words.

GRRRR ... I'M THE BIG, BAD WOLF. FEAR ME!

Q Which elf is the best singer?

A Elf-is Presley.

RIDDLE ✷ ME THIS

What is light as a feather, but Hercules can't hold it for five minutes?

His breath.

Q How are Greek towels labeled?

A His and Her-cules.

HERACLES: All three of Cerberus's heads get along so well!

PERSEPHONE: Yes, they have a special connection.

Q What did Poseidon say to the sea monster?

A "What's Kraken?"

Q What kind of footwear does a Greek god wear?

A Tennis Zeus.

Q What does a unicorn put on its corn dog?

A Pega-sauce.

Beluga whales can change the shape of their heads by blowing air into their sinuses.

KNOCK, KNOCK.

Who's there?
Open says.
Open says who?
Open says me!

Q Where did Humpty Dumpty get a manufacturing job?

HUMPTY DUMPTY RESUME

A In an eggplant.

TONGUE TWISTER!

Say this fast three times:

Clumsy clowns crushed the king's crown.

Q What is a unicorn's best friend?

A A corn dog.

Q How do you brush a dragon's teeth?

A Very carefully.

Q What kind of dreams does Goldilocks have?

A Night-bears.

Q What do you call a **pretty person** with a **broom?**

A Sweeping Beauty.

CINDERELLA: I made you a numbered list to take to the grocery store with you. Did you take it?

PRINCE CHARMING: Yes, and I think I picked up everything it said to get.

CINDERELLA: Why do you have so many bags? What did you get?

PRINCE CHARMING: 1 pepper, 2 zucchinis, 3 tea bags, 4 loaves of bread, 5 turkeys, and 6 pumpkins.

Q Why did the Cyclops give up his teaching job?

A Because he only had one pupil.

199

LOL

MYTHS & FABLES

In earlier versions of the **Rumpelstiltskin** fairy tale, he escapes on a **flying** LADLE.

Half of **Iceland's** population **believe** in the existence of **fairies, elves,** and **trolls** called *HULDUFÓLK.*

GELOS was the **GREEK GOD** of laughter.

In the **1960s, BIGFOOT** was placed on **Russia's ENDANGERED SPECIES** list.

BIG FOOT XING

DUE TO SIGHTINGS IN THE AREA OF A CREATURE RESEMBLING "BIG FOOT" THIS SIGN HAS BEEN POSTED FOR YOUR SAFETY

IN CALIFORNIA, U.S.A., A **PONY** DRESSED AS A **UNICORN** ONCE LED **POLICE** ON AN HOURS-LONG **CHASE.**

APPEARANCES CORN BE DECEIVING.

CHAPTER 8

Uproarious Dinosaurs

HA!HA!HA!HA!HA!
HA!HA!HA!
HA!HA!

KNOCK, KNOCK.

Who's there?
Dinosaurs.
Dinosaurs who?
No, dinosaurs don't who, they roar.

Fossils aren't always bones. Scientists have discovered fossils of dinosaur footprints, eggs, feathers, and even poop!

Q Where does a *Triceratops* sit?

A On its Tricera-bottom.

Q What's as **BIG** as a **dinosaur** but weighs **less** than one?

A A dinosaur's shadow.

Q Which swimming dinosaur has the best manners?

PARDON ME, YOU LOOK VERY NICE TODAY.

A The Please-iosaurus.

Did you know that *Diplodocus* was **88 feet** (27 m) **long?** That's almost the **length** of an **NBA basketball court.**

Its neck made up around 20 feet (6 m) of that length.

DINOSAUR 1:
Do you like flying dinosaur puns?
DINOSAUR 2:
No, they are ptero-ble.

TONGUE 🌀 **TWISTER!**

Say this fast three times:

Diplodocus **hocus-pocus.**

PACHYCEPHALOSAURUS MOM:
Bring an umbrella to school, it's raining.
PACHYCEPHALOSAURUS KID:
No, I don't want to.
PACHYCEPHALOSAURUS MOM:
Ugh, you have such a hard head.

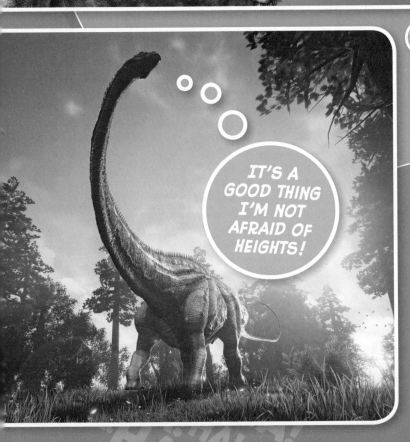

IT'S A GOOD THING I'M NOT AFRAID OF HEIGHTS!

Q What do you get if you cross a wizard and a *Gigantosaurus?*

A dinosaur-cerer.

A

205

Q Why did tyrannosaurs fight with their teeth?

A Because none of them could win an arm wrestling match.

Q Why did the *Spinosaurus* eat an automobile?

A Because it was a car-nivore.

Q What kind of dinosaur is the fastest?

A A Pronto-saurus.

PTERODACTYL 1: Can you fly high?
PTERODACTYL 2: I can really saur!

Q What is a dentist's favorite dinosaur?

A The Flossa-raptor.

Q What does a dinosaur wear to a wedding?

A A Tricera-top hat.

Q What kind of dinosaurs like scary movies?

A Terror-dactyls.

Q How did the *Herrerasaurus* feel after its first day at the gym?

A Dino-sore.

Q Which dinosaur shouldn't get wet?

A A Stegosau-rust.

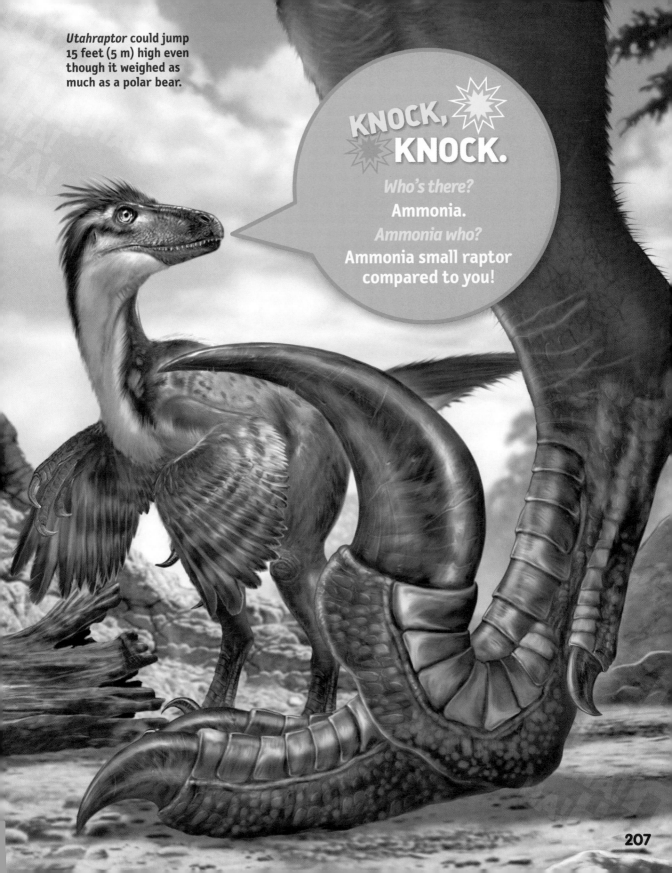

Utahraptor could jump 15 feet (5 m) high even though it weighed as much as a polar bear.

KNOCK, KNOCK.

Who's there?
Ammonia.
Ammonia who?
Ammonia small raptor compared to you!

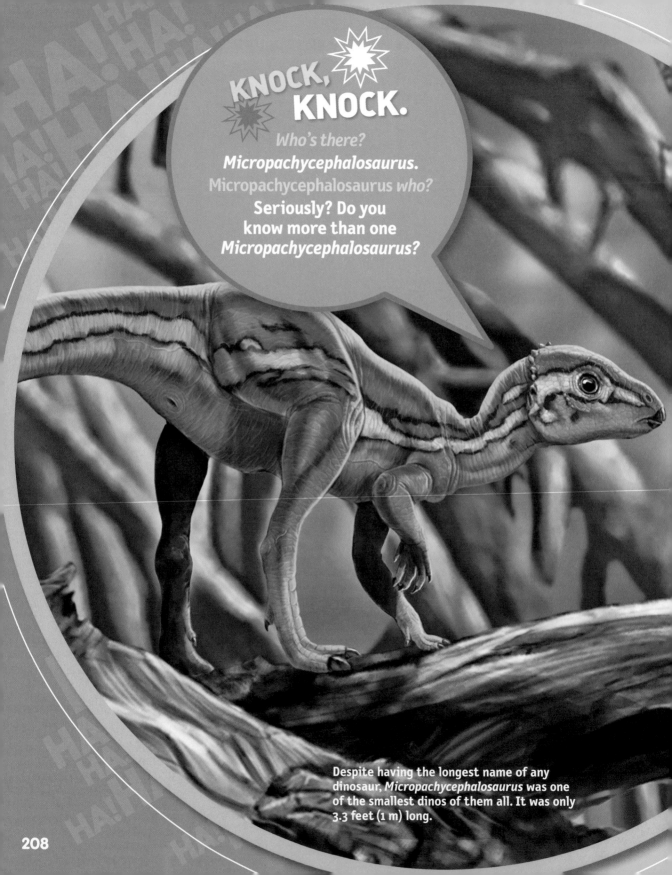

KNOCK, KNOCK.

Who's there?
Micropachycephalosaurus.
Micropachycephalosaurus who?
Seriously? Do you know more than one *Micropachycephalosaurus?*

Despite having the longest name of any dinosaur, *Micropachycephalosaurus* was one of the smallest dinos of them all. It was only 3.3 feet (1 m) long.

Q Why did the dinosaur paint itself different colors?

A So it could hide in a crayon box.

Q Why did *Allosaurus* eat its food raw?

A Because it didn't know how to cook.

Q What do you get when a dinosaur **sneezes?**

A Out of the way!

Q Where do dinosaurs sunbathe?

A At the dino-shore.

ALLOSAURUS MOM: Ssshhh, your father is sleeping!
ALLOSAURUS KID: I know, I can hear the dino-snores.

Q What do you get if you cross a termite and an *Ankylosaurus*?

A Dino-mite.

TONGUE TWISTER!

Say this fast three times:

Ornithomimus is behind us.

HAVE I GOT ANYTHING STUCK IN MY TEETH?

Q What do you get if you cross a mythical flying horse and a spiky dinosaur?

A A Pega-saurus.

209

SAY WHAT?

NAME **Nibbler**

FAVORITE ACTIVITY **Snacking on the run**

FAVORITE FOOD **Anything I can sink my teeth into**

PET PEEVE **Flossing**

DINOSAUR PUNS ARE PTER-ABLE!

The name *Spinosaurus* means "spine lizard." *Spinosaurus* was the largest carnivorous dinosaur on Earth.

WHERE DOES AN APATOSAURUS EAT? ANYWHERE IT WANTS TO.

What do you call a *Velociraptor* in high heels?

A My-feet-are-saurus.

Q

What's the difference between a *Conchoraptor* and a carrot?

A A carrot is orange.

NO BONES ABOUT IT, EXTINCTION IS THE PITS.

Q

What's green and hangs from trees?

A Dinosaur snot.

KID: Why are all these dinosaur bones so old?
TEACHER: I guess they can't afford new ones.
KID: Will they ever get more bones?
TEACHER: That remains to be seen.

THE *T. REX* FAMILY:

- ☐ Nervous rex: scared to ride the big roller coasters
- ☐ T. wrecks: destroys every toy he gets
- ☐ Tea rex: refuses to drink coffee
- ☐ Tyrannosaurus flex: loves to go to the gym but usually skips arm days

Did you know that although the name means **"three-**horned face," *Triceratops* had only **two proper horns?**

The third "horn" was made out of soft proteins, and scientists aren't sure what its purpose was.

RIDDLE ✸ ME THIS

What is easy for a baby *Brachiosaurus* to get into, but difficult to get out of?

⅂rouble. *(Trouble.)*

DINOSAUR 1: Who stepped on your foot?
DINOSAUR 2: See that *Apatosaurus* over there?
DINOSAUR 1: Yes.
DINOSAUR 2: Well, I didn't.

Q

What do you get if you cross a dinosaur and a mouse?

Giant holes in your baseboards. *(inverted answer)*

A

A FATHER AND SON *BRACHIOSAURUS* were eating dinner one day and the son asked, "Dad, are we herbivores?"

"Yes, son. Now eat your dinner," his father replied.

"But if we are herbivores, that means we don't eat bugs, right?" the son asked.

The father sighed, "Yes, son, we don't eat bugs—only plants. Now stop asking questions and eat your dinner."

"But, Dad, are you SURE we don't eat bugs? Are there any kinds of bugs we DO eat?" he asked again.

"Listen!" the father yelled. "I've told you already, we don't eat any kind of bug. We can talk about this after we finish our leaves."

After dinner, the father dino asked, "Now, what is it about eating bugs you wanted to ask me?"

"OH, NEVER MIND," the younger dino said. "There was a large beetle on your leaves but it's gone now."

Cats greet each other by touching noses.

KNOCK, KNOCK.

Who's there?

Raptor.

Raptor who?

Raptor presents, I'm ready for the party!

Q Which **dinosaur** was the most trustworthy?

A The *Troodon.*

Q Why did the *Archaeopteryx* catch the worm?

A Because it was an early bird.

Q What do you call a dinosaur with one eye?

A Eye-saur.

Q What makes more noise than one *Iguanodon?*

A Two *Iguanodons.*

Q What game does an *Apatosaurus* and a *Compsognathus* play together?

A Squash.

Q Why didn't the *Argentinosaurus* cross the road?

A Because there weren't any roads back then.

Q What has a **spiked tail, giant plates** on its back, and **16 wheels?**

A A *Stegosaurus* on roller skates.

Q Which **dinosaur** never got lost?

A A Map-usaurus.

PALEONTOLOGIST 1: Hey! I think I found a dino skeleton!
PALEONTOLOGIST 2: Nope, fossil-arm.

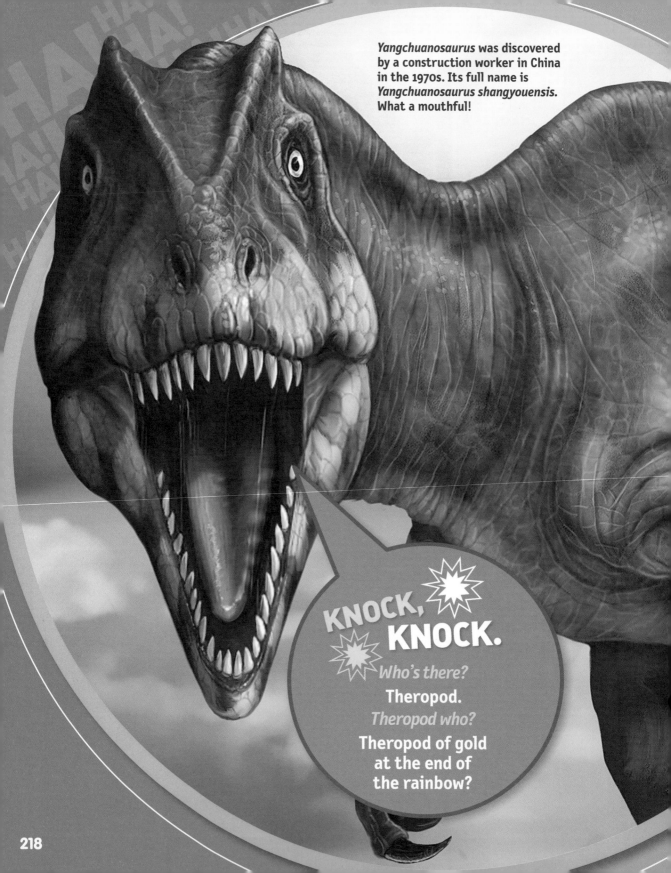

Yangchuanosaurus was discovered by a construction worker in China in the 1970s. Its full name is *Yangchuanosaurus shangyouensis*. What a mouthful!

KNOCK, KNOCK.
Who's there?
Theropod.
Theropod who?
Theropod of gold at the end of the rainbow?

218

Q When can three theropods fit under one umbrella and not get wet?

A When it isn't raining.

Q What is a *T. rex*'s least favorite song?

A "If you're happy and you know it, clap your hands."

Q What did a *Megalosaurus* have that no other dinosaur had?

A A baby *Megalosaurus*.

Q What do you call a dinosaur who loves to eat?

A An om-nom-nom-nomivore.

Q Which kind of **dinosaur** performs **pop music?**

A A rap-tor.

KID: Do you know any good dinosaur authors?
LIBRARIAN: Well, you could try Sarah Tops.

Q What's worse than an **elephant** with an **ear infection?**

A A *Diplodocus* with a sore throat.

Q Why were **dinosaurs hipsters?**

A Because they existed before it was cool.

Q **What followed the *Allosaurus?***

A Its tail.

219

Q

What do you call it when an *Albertosaurus* slides into home plate?

Q

Why are **dinosaur fossils** so **memorable?**

A

Because they know how to make an impression.

ANDERSON:
An *Apatosaurus* just ate a shoe factory!
MIA:
I'm not surprised, they're plant-eaters.

CHIHUAHUA-SAURUS REX STRIKES FEAR IN THE HEARTS OF HUMANS EVERYWHERE!

FOSSIL 1:
How did you meet your wife?
FOSSIL 2:
On a carbon dating site.

RIDDLE ☀ ☀ ME THIS

What are **two things** an *Apatosaurus* can **never** eat for **breakfast?**

Lunch and dinner.

A dino-score.

Did you know that the **smallest dino** in North America weighed less than a **teacup Chihuahua**?

Fruitadens haagarorum was just 28 inches (71 cm) long and weighed less than two pounds (0.9 kg).

VELOCIRAPTOR 1: I was so hungry I just ate my pillow.
VELOCIRAPTOR 2: I thought you looked a little down in the mouth.

Q

Which plant-eating **dinosaur** can you always find in the **backyard?**

The Iguano-lawn.

A

Q

What do you get if you cross a dinosaur and a chicken?

Tyrannosaurus pecks. **A**

MY SELFIES NEVER TURN OUT RIGHT.

NAMES
Spike and Chomper

FAVORITE ACTIVITY
Lurking in swamps

FAVORITE FOOD
Anything chewy

PET PEEVE
Fast food

SHOULD I CALL YOU? OR SEND A TYRANNOSAURUS TEXT?

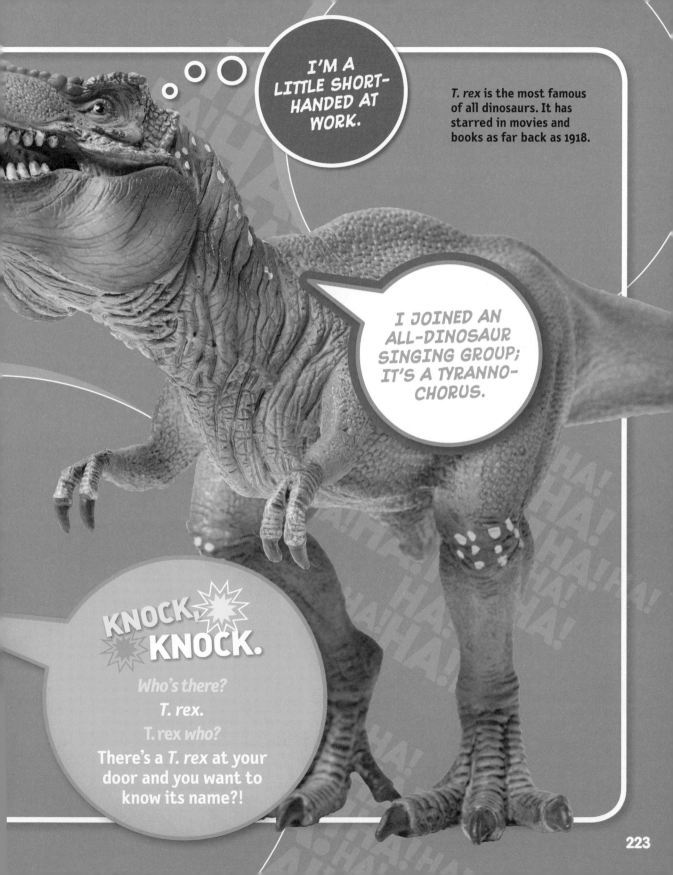

I'M A LITTLE SHORT-HANDED AT WORK.

T. rex is the most famous of all dinosaurs. It has starred in movies and books as far back as 1918.

I JOINED AN ALL-DINOSAUR SINGING GROUP; IT'S A TYRANNO-CHORUS.

KNOCK KNOCK.
Who's there?
T. rex.
T. rex who?
There's a T. rex at your door and you want to know its name?!

223

KNOCK, KNOCK.

Who's there?
Jurassic.
Jurassic who?
If Jurassic you should go lie down.

It's believed that *T. rex* could eat up to 500 pounds (227 kg) of meat in one bite!

Q Where did the paleontologist find the dinosaur bones?

A In a foss-hill.

Q What do you get if you cross a **dinosaur** and a **pickle?**

A A Dill-ophosaurus.

Q What was the most indecisive dinosaur?

A The Stay-go-saurus.

DAVE: What family does the *T. rex* belong to?
MAGGIE: I don't think families in our neighborhood have one.

Q Why can't you hear a **pterosaur** using the **bathroom?**

A Because the *p* is silent.

I REALLY KNOW HOW TO MAKE A GREAT IMPRESSION.

PORT-O-DON

225

226

Q Why was the *Stegosaurus* such a good volleyball player?

A Because it could really spike the ball.

Oviraptor's name means "egg stealer" although it has been proved that it wasn't an egg thief at all.

Q What do you get if you cross a pig and a *Brachiosaurus*?

A Jurassic Pork.

PABLO: I lost my *Apatosaurus*.
SAMI: Why don't you put an ad in the newspaper?
PABLO: Don't be silly, dinosaurs can't read.

LOST DINO

Q What's a *T. rex*'s **least** favorite exercise?

A Push-ups.

TAG! YOU'RE IT!

Q How do you greet a large **theropod**?

A "Allosaurus!"

Q What do you call a **paleontologist** who **sleeps** all the time?

A Lazy bones.

227

LOL DINOSAURS

There is a town in Colorado, U.S.A., called **Dinosaur.** Some of its STREET NAMES include **STEGOSAURUS FREEWAY** and **TYRANNOSAURUS TRAIL.**

Rhinorex was named for its **giant schnoz.** Its name is Latin for **"KING NOSE."**

Sauropods, or **long-necked dinosaurs,** are believed to have **PASSED GAS** constantly.

ARE WE THERE YET?

Paleontologists were **SO ANNOYED** while trying to **RECONSTRUCT** the **FOSSILIZED HEAD** of a newly discovered dinosaur that they named the dino **Irritator.**

I NEVER FALL BEHIND ON MY SCHOOLWORK.

WHEN *STEGOSAURUS* WAS DISCOVERED, SCIENTISTS THOUGHT IT HAD A SECOND BRAIN IN ITS REAR END.

CHAPTER 9

Amusing Music

HA!HA!HA!HA!HA!
HA!HA!HA!HA!
HA!HA!
HA!HA!HA!

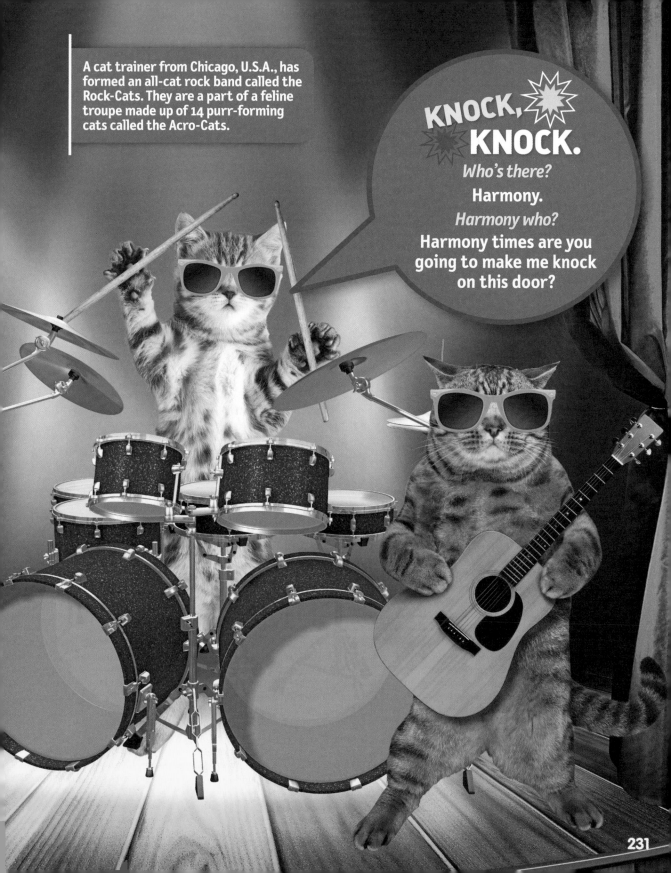

A cat trainer from Chicago, U.S.A., has formed an all-cat rock band called the Rock-Cats. They are a part of a feline troupe made up of 14 purr-forming cats called the Acro-Cats.

KNOCK, KNOCK.

Who's there?

Harmony.

Harmony who?

Harmony times are you going to make me knock on this door?

How do **composers** remember what to get at the **grocery store?**

LAUGHABLE ≡LIST≡

TERRIBLE BAND NAMES:

- ☐ The Do-You-Think-They-Can-Hear-Us Trio
- ☐ Tone Deaf and the Pitches: an a cappella group
- ☐ Rusty Trumpet and the Squeakers
- ☐ Wind and the Tooter: a bagpipe and horn duet

LET'S TRY THIS AGAIN FROM THE TOP ...

WE REALLY WANT TO SHOW THEM HOW WELL WE CAN DO THE CHICKEN DANCE.

TRACEY: I was going to tell you a joke about composers but I'm afraid you can't Handel it.
CATHIE: Call me Bach if you change your mind.

Q

Why are snakes naturally musical?

A

Because they have scales.

TONGUE TWISTER!

Say this fast three times:

A **tutor** who **tooted** the flute, tried to **tutor** two **tooters** to **toot.**

Q Why didn't the wolf want to sing in a band?

A He only knew how to howl.

Did you know that **scientists** have developed technology that analyzes the **sounds** that **chickens** make?

The software can determine the difference between the calls of healthy and sick birds.

ROBERTO: Did you hear about the grizzly that was booed off the stage at the open mic night?
GARRY: No! Was he any good?
ROBERTO: His singing was unbearable.

Q What do you get if you cross an origami teacher and a singer?

A Rapping paper.

Q What is a **composer's** favorite **vegetable?**

A Bach-choy.

Q What's a skeleton's favorite instrument?

A The trom-bone.

Q How do you **catch** a **bassoon?**

A With a clari-net.

Q What do you call a dad who raps?

A A hip-pop.

Q What kind of germs do you find in a composer's fridge?

A Bach-teria.

Q Why did the **singer** **break** **into song?**

A Because she couldn't find the key.

Q What do you get if you cross a sweet potato and a musician?

A A yam session.

MUSIC TEACHER: Billy, why are you bringing a ladder to our singing lesson?

BILLY: To help me reach the high notes.

Q What has a **trunk,** lots of **keys,** and **four legs?**

A A piano stuck in a tree.

Q What kind of band can't play music?

A A rubber band.

Q What's a golfer's favorite type of music?

A Swing.

234

KNOCK, KNOCK.

Who's there?
Sing.
Sing who?
Whoooooooooo!

De Brazza's monkeys have excellent hiding skills, which makes getting an accurate count of how many live in the wild very difficult.

KNOCK, KNOCK.

Who's there?
Arthur.
Arthur who?
Arthur any earplugs around? This band is terrible.

236

Q What kind of music do mummies perform?

A Wrap.

Q What song do you sing at a snowman's birthday party?

A "Freeze a Jolly Good Fellow."

Q What kind of candy plays in the horn section of the orchestra?

A A tooty fruity.

MUSIC TEACHER: Please tune in your homework.
HIRO: I don't have it, I forgot my notebook.
MUSIC TEACHER: Now you're really in treble.
HIRO: I know, it wasn't very clef-er of me.

Giraffes can grow to be 18 feet (6 m) tall. You don't want this guy standing in front of you at a concert!

Q What is Tarzan's favorite Christmas song?

A "Jungle Bells."

OOOO ... I LOVE BELTING OUT MY FAVORITE SONG!

Q What keeps jazz musicians on Earth?

A Groovity.

Q Why did the turkey join the rock band?

A Because he had the drumsticks.

MUSIC HISTORIAN: The composer Handel didn't ever go shopping.
STUDENT: Why not?
MUSIC HISTORIAN: Because he was baroque.

SAY WHAT?

NAME
Lionel

FAVORITE HANGOUT
Mane Street

FAVORITE BAND
The Catstreet Boys

PET PEEVE
Copycats

IF A FISH CAN'T SING, THEY CAN USE AUTO-TUNA.

BARITONES BRING ME DOWN.

I LIKE TO SING SOPRANO— IT LEAVES MY LISTENERS ON A HIGH NOTE.

An adult male lion's roar can be heard from five miles (8 km) away. He definitely doesn't need a microphone to sing.

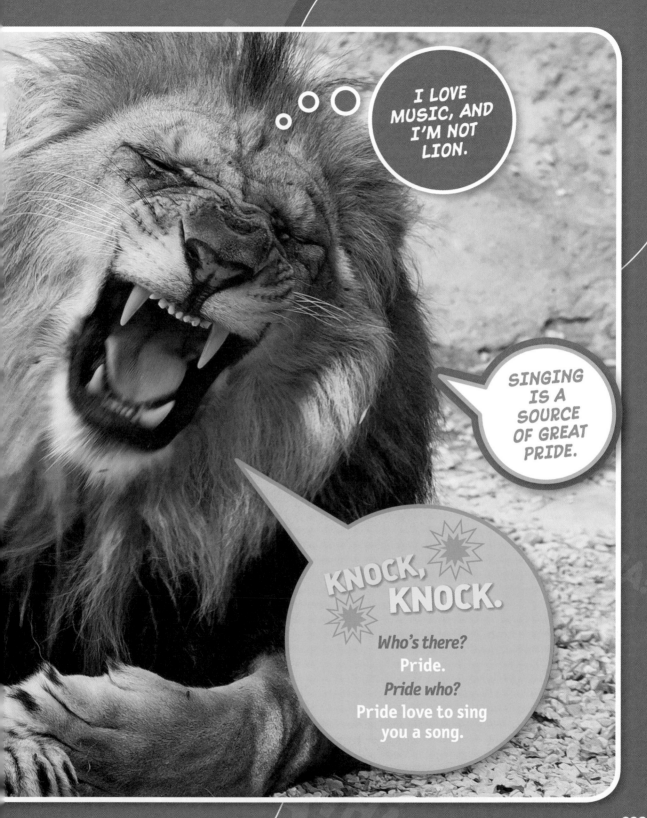

What instrument do you keep in the bathroom?

A A toilet paper tuba.

Q **Which pet makes the most noise?**

A A trum-pet.

RIDDLE ✷ **ME THIS**

What instrument can be played and heard but never seen?

Your voice.

Q **What do you call a lizard that likes hip-hop music?**

A A rap-tile.

CAROL: I brought my tuba for show-and-tell.
TEACHER: Can you hold it up so we can all see it?
CAROL: I can't lift it!
TEACHER: That's what I call heavy metal music.

LA LA LAAAAA LA LA

HEY! KEEP IT DOWN! I'M TRYING TO SLEEP IN HERE! WERE YOU BORN IN A BARN?

Did you know that a **pig** rescued by the SPCA in British Columbia, Canada, would make **melodic vocalizations** when he saw his favorite volunteer?

They called him Lyle the Singing Pig of Surrey.

Q

What do you get if you cross **classical music** and a **boy band?**

Bach Street Boys.

A

LESLIE: Oh no! I broke my tuba!
VICTORIA: Don't worry, I have a tuba glue.

PIANO TUNER: I've come to tune the piano.
MUSIC TEACHER: I didn't call you.
PIANO TUNER: No, the people who live next door did.

A BIOLOGY TEACHER TAKES HIS DAUGHTER TO HER ORGAN PERFORMANCE.

When it's her turn to play, she walks out on stage, turns to the audience, and says, "I'd like to thank my father for teaching me everything I know. He is so talented and I'd love for him to perform with me."

Her father is touched and runs up on stage with her.

243

KNOCK, KNOCK.

Who's there?
Allison.
Allison who?
Allison to the music on the radio.

A zoo in Australia released a music single created by an orangutan named Kluet. The song was recorded on a smartphone music app.

Q What do **composers** take when they have a **sore throat?**

A Tchi-cough-sky-drops.

Q What do you get if you put a radio in the freezer?

A Cool music.

Q What song did one octopus sing to the other?

A "I wanna hold your hand, hand, hand, hand, hand, hand, hand, hand."

Q Why are **pianos hard** to **open?**

A Because the keys are inside.

Q Why did the girl decide to become an opera singer?

A Because the opera-tunity came up.

Q What **instrument** does a **fisherman** play?

A The bass guitar.

Q What do you do if you **can't find** someone to **sing with?**

A Duet yourself.

FARMER 1:
I taught my horse to play the violin.
FARMER 2:
Is she good at it?
FARMER 1:
She sure is, she's going to be in a musical!
FARMER 2:
Which one?
FARMER 1:
Fiddler on the Hoof.

Q What is a trombone's favorite playground equipment?

A The slide.

245

KNOCK, KNOCK.

Who's there?
Cymbals.
Cymbals who?
**Cymbals have horns
and others don't.**

A female snowy owl will sit on
her eggs for a month until they
hatch. A male snowy owl will
bring her food during this time.

Q What is Beethoven's favorite fruit?

A Ba-na-na-naaa.

Q What has **40 feet** and **sings**?

A A choir.

Q Why **shouldn't** you trust a **harp**?

A Because sometimes they're lyres.

Q Why did the pianist bang the side of his head against the keys?

A He wanted to play by ear.

Q How do you know when a musician has left the house?

A He leaves a note.

OPERA SINGER 1: Why did you jump in the ocean with your dress on?
OPERA SINGER 2: Because I'm a deep C diva!

RIDDLE ✹ ME THIS

At the **sound** of me, people sometimes **stamp their feet** and **wave their arms**, and sometimes they may **laugh** or **weep**. What am I?

Music.

I'M NOT READY FOR OPEN MIC NIGHT! WHAT WAS I THINKING?!

Q What do composers put on their pizzas?

A Mozart-rella cheese.

Some people listen to
dolphin sounds set to
music to meditate.

What is full of keys but can't open any doors?

A piano.

Q Why are icy sidewalks like music?

A If you don't C sharp, you'll B-flat.

STEPHEN: Yuck! I was singing in the shower and got shampoo in my mouth.

ANNA: Oh, I love a good soap opera!

Q What's **yellow**, weighs **1,000 pounds**, and **sings?**

A Two 500-pound canaries.

Q Why did the kid's tortilla chips start dancing?

A Because he put some salsa music on.

MUSICIAN 1: Wow, the conductor is really angry with us.

MUSICIAN 2: He is totally having a tempo-tantrum.

Q What kind of soap does a composer use?

A Anti-Bach-terial.

I CAN'T READ SHEET MUSIC; I PLAY BY EAR.

Q What do you call a **musical insect?**

A A hum-bug.

SAY WHAT?

NAMES
Rock and Roll

FAVORITE ACTIVITY
Shaking our hips

FAVORITE DANCE
Hippo-Hop

PET PEEVE
Hippo-critical people

THESE JOKES REALLY STRUCK A CHORD.

BE CAREFUL, MUSIC PUNS WILL GET YOU IN TREBLE.

THOSE WHO DON'T LIKE THESE MUSIC PUNS HAVE MY SYMPHONY.

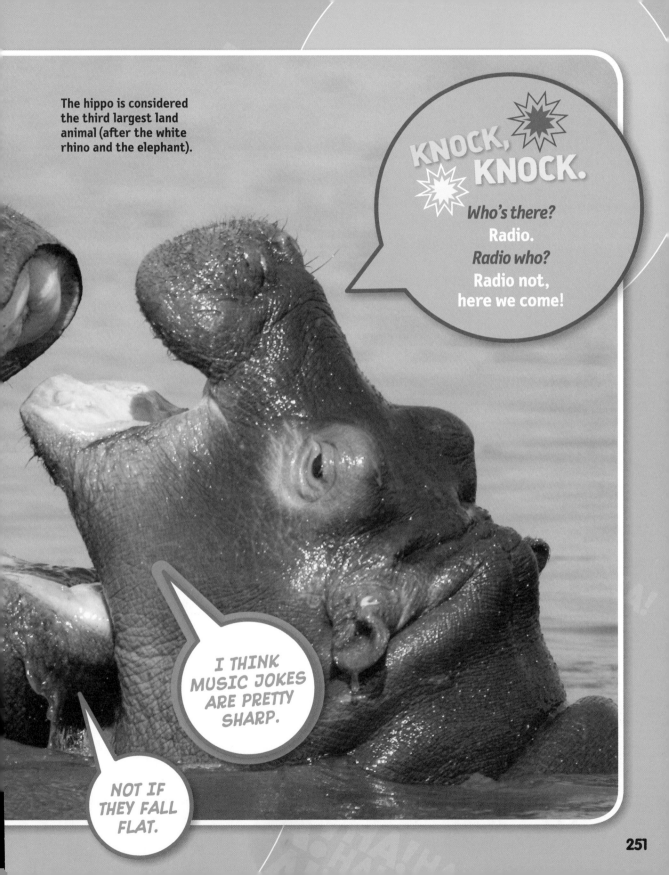

The hippo is considered the third largest land animal (after the white rhino and the elephant).

There are 264 species of monkeys that are divided into two groups: Old World (which live in Africa and Asia) and New World (which live in South America).

KNOCK, KNOCK.
Who's there?
Turnip.
Turnip who?
Turnip the volume, this is my favorite song!

HMM HMM HMMM ... IF YOU DON'T KNOW THE WORDS, JUST HUM ALONG.

Q What do you call a **musician** who was **petrified** by **Medusa?**

A A rock star.

Q What do you get if you cross a **lamp** and a **violin?**

A Light music.

RIDDLE ❋ ME THIS

If an **orchestra** is playing outside in a **thunderstorm,** which **member** is most likely to get struck by **lightning?**

The conductor.

Q Why are cats such good singers?

A Because they are naturally mew-sical.

Q What do ghosts bring to their music lessons?

A Sheet music.

Q Why didn't the llama like to perform with a band?

A She enjoyed singing alpaca-pella.

Q Why did the **recliner** learn to play the **guitar?**

A Because it was a rocking chair.

DAD: Why aren't string instruments good at puzzles?
DAUGHTER: I don't know, why?
DAD: Because violins never solve anything.

253

LOL
MUSIC

A **SONG** that gets **stuck** in your **head** is called an **EARWORM**.

A band sent a **piece of pizza** into **SPACE** as part of a **music video.**

The **first musical comedy,** *The Black Domino/ Between You, Me, and the Post,* was **performed** on **Broadway** in **1878.**

Members of a **marching band** in **Michigan, U.S.A.,** dress as **CLOWNS** while **performing.**

MUSICAL CANINE FREESTYLE

IS A SPORT WHERE **HUMANS** AND **DOGS** PERFORM A ROUTINE TOGETHER. IT COMBINES **DANCE, TRICKS,** AND **OBEDIENCE** TRAINING.

I'M NOT A GREAT DANCER ... I HAVE TWO LEFT FEET.

CHAPTER 10

Riotous Riches

HA!HA!HA!HA!HA!HA!
HA!HA!HA!HA!
HA!HA!

In the 18th century, the value of a coin was determined by its weight in gold or silver. Sometimes a coin would be cut into smaller pieces for payment or to make change.

KNOCK, KNOCK.

Who's there?
Needle.
Needle who?
Needle little help carrying this treasure!

STEPHEN: I just don't understand how gems are formed.

ANNA: Really? It's crystal clear to me!

LAUGHABLE LIST

TERRIBLE PIRATE NAMES:

- ☐ Captain Seasick
- ☐ William the Wavering
- ☐ Scurvy Teeth McGee
- ☐ Fear O' the Sea
- ☐ Sinky McSharkbait

GEOLOGIST 1: How did you become an expert on sinkholes?

GEOLOGIST 2: Oh, I just sort of fell into it.

THESE AREN'T DIAMONDS, THEY'RE RHINO-STONES.

Q

Which is the richest fish?

A A goldfish.

TONGUE TWISTER!

Say this fast three times:

A proper copper coffee pot.

Q Why did the jewel thief steal a snake from the zoo?

A The sign said it was a diamondback.

Did you know that a **group** of **rhinos** is called a **crash?** Crashes are made up of a female and her calves.

Rhinos are an endangered species. It's estimated there are only around 29,000 of them left in the wild.

Q What's a **pirate's** favorite subject in school?

A Arrrr.

Q What did the pirate say at the end of his 79th year?

A "Aye, Matey."

ARCHAEOLOGIST 1: I just found a tomb of a mummified pharaoh!
ARCHAEOLOGIST 2: Are you serious?
ARCHAEOLOGIST 1: No bones about it!

Q Who did the **archaeologist talk to** when he was **sad?**

A His mummy.

TONGUE TWISTER!

Say this fast three times:

Penny's pretty pink piggy bank.

ANCIENT EGYPTIAN 1: Ouch, my back is sore from storing all these treasures in pharaoh's tomb.

ANCIENT EGYPTIAN 2: Maybe you should visit the Cairo-practor.

Q Where do birds invest their money?

A In the stork market.

Q Who stole the **expensive soap** from the bathtub?

A The robber duckie.

Q What do you call **money** made of **clay?**

A Play-Dough.

Q What happens when you throw a blue sapphire into the Red Sea?

A It gets wet.

Q Why did the priceless painting go to jail?

A It was framed.

Q Why did the gold prospector call in sick at work?

A He had gold fever.

260

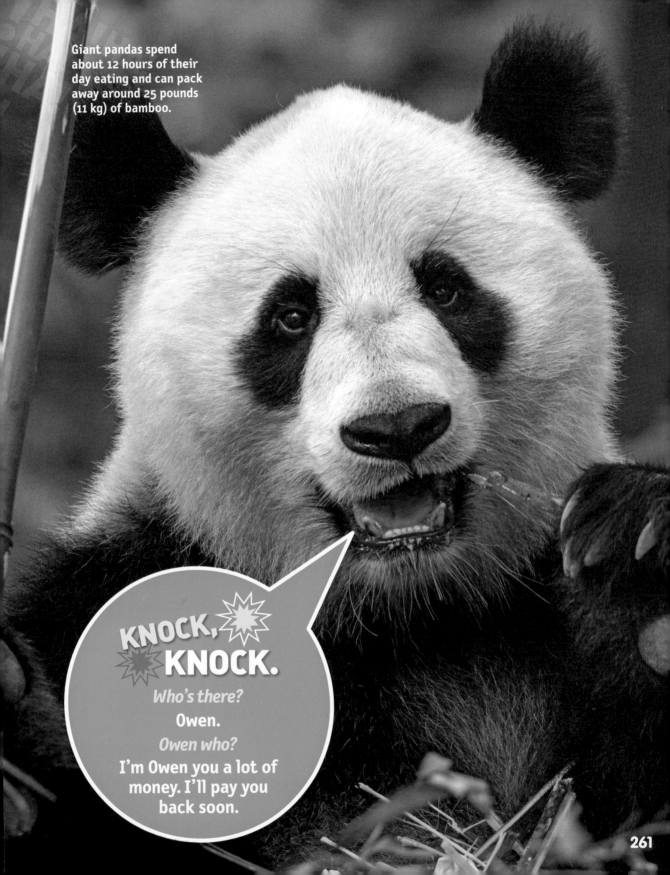

Giant pandas spend about 12 hours of their day eating and can pack away around 25 pounds (11 kg) of bamboo.

KNOCK, KNOCK.

Who's there?

Owen.

Owen who?

I'm Owen you a lot of money. I'll pay you back soon.

KNOCK, KNOCK.

Who's there?
Archie.
Archie who?
Archie-ologists have found some amazing treasures.

A macaw has a bone in its tongue that helps the bird open up fruits and nuts.

Q What do you call it when a dog swallows a wedding ring?

A A diamond in the ruff.

Q Why did the thief take a bath after stealing the royal jewels?

A So he could make a clean getaway.

Q What do you call a pirate who skips school?

A Captain Hooky.

Q What did the **pirate** use to keep his **parrot** on his shoulder?

A Polly-grip.

I'M SURE I CAN DIG UP A GEM OF A JOKE TO TELL YOU. OF QUARTZ, I HOPE IT ISN'T AN EMER-OLD ONE.

PIRATE: Can you take a look at the moles on me back?
DOCTOR: There's nothing to worry about, they're benign.
PIRATE: Shiver me timbers! When I spied them this morning, there be only four!

RIDDLE ME THIS

What has a **head**, a **tail**, no legs, and is **brown?**

A penny.

Q What do you eat to get rich?

A Fortune cookies.

Q What did the robber say when he held up the pizzeria?

A "Gimme all your dough."

SAY WHAT?

People have been keeping goldfish as pets for more than 2,000 years.

NAMES Goldie, Bubbles, Doubloon, and Bill

FAVORITE ACTIVITY Fishing for compliments

FAVORITE GAME Salmon Says

PET PEEVE Bowls

WE ARE O-FISH-ALLY FABULOUS!

I KEEP MY MONEY IN A RIVERBANK.

Q Why did the pirate buy a baby chick instead of a parrot?

PRICE $1⁰⁰

A Because it was going cheep.

Q Why didn't the **quarter** roll down the hill with the **nickel?**

A Because it had more cents.

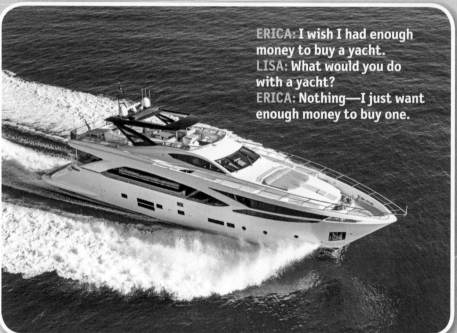

ERICA: I wish I had enough money to buy a yacht.
LISA: What would you do with a yacht?
ERICA: Nothing—I just want enough money to buy one.

LAUGHABLE LIST

HOW TO TELL IF YOUR TREASURE IS FAKE:

☐ Your gold coins have chocolate inside.
☐ Your treasure chest is made of papier-mâché.
☐ Your diamonds bounce.
☐ You were in a toy store when you "discovered" it.
☐ Your diamonds and jewels smell like fruit flavors.

Q What kind of lipstick do pirates wear?

A Ship gloss.

Did you know that a **bunny's teeth** never stop growing? They have to chew on wood or hay to keep them **worn down.**

Babies are born with their eyes closed and no fur.

THIS ISN'T THE TYPE OF CARAT I WAS TALKING ABOUT.

SOPHIA: I'm one step away from being rich!
FRANCESCO: Really?!
SOPHIA: Yep, all I need is lots of money!

MUMMY 1: Wow! Look at all these treasures they buried us with!
MUMMY 2: Shhh ... let's keep it under wraps.

Q Why did the man put his money in the freezer?

A He wanted some cold hard cash.

267

CAPTAIN SHIPWRECK THE PIRATE wrote a letter to his longtime pirate friend, Scurvy McChumbucket:

Dear Scurvy, I've been traveling the sea for many years and have just hauled the largest booty of my life! I have more emeralds and rubies than I can count. I hope you are well, please write to me soon.

Two months passed and his friend didn't respond. Years passed and Shipwreck sent Scurvy many more letters, but he never received a reply.

One day while docked, he spotted Scurvy and rushed over to see him. "Scurvy, my old pirate friend! I'm so happy to see you! I've written you so many letters, but why haven't you responded?"

Scurvy replied, "I prefer to talk aye to aye."

The southern elephant seal is massive! It can grow up to 20 feet (6 m) long and can weigh up to 8,800 pounds (3,992 kg).

KNOCK, KNOCK.

Who's there?
Barry.
Barry who?
Barry the treasure where no one will find it!

Q Why did the baker sell her yeast?

A To make some dough.

Q Why do bankers go to the movies by themselves?

A Because they're loaners.

Q What did the ceiling say to the diamond chandelier?

A You light up my life.

Q Why did the belt go to jail?

A It held up a pair of pants.

Q Why did the spider buy a fancy sports car?

A So he could take it for a spin.

Q What does a wasp wear when it goes to the bank to deposit its fortunes?

A A buzz-ness suit.

BUSINESS WOMAN: I have an idea that will double your money instantly.

INVESTOR: Really? Here's $100, what do I do?

BUSINESS WOMAN: Fold it in half.

Q What's the most expensive air?

A A millionaire.

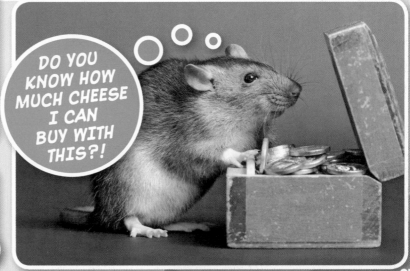

DO YOU KNOW HOW MUCH CHEESE I CAN BUY WITH THIS?!

Baby goats can stand within minutes of being born.

KNOCK, KNOCK.

Who's there?
Garden.
Garden who?
Garden these gold coins with my life.

Q What did the solid gold plate say to the jeweled goblet?

A "Dinner's on me."

Q What do you call a **fake Irish diamond?**

A A sham-rock.

Q Where can you see mummies and the treasures of the ancient Egyptian cows?

A At the history moooooseum.

Q When does it rain money?

A If there's a change in the weather.

SCULPTOR: I'll need the diamonds we are embedding into the statue by Thursday.
JEWELER: Can we change it to Friday?
SCULPTOR: Sorry, it's set in stone.

Q Where did the **chandelier** go to **dance?**

A The Crystal Ball.

Q How do you **secure** a **jewelry store?**

A You locket.

Q What did the gold say to the pyrite?

A "You're a fool!"

POLLY'S IN CHARGE NOW! CRACKERS WHENEVER I WANT!

273

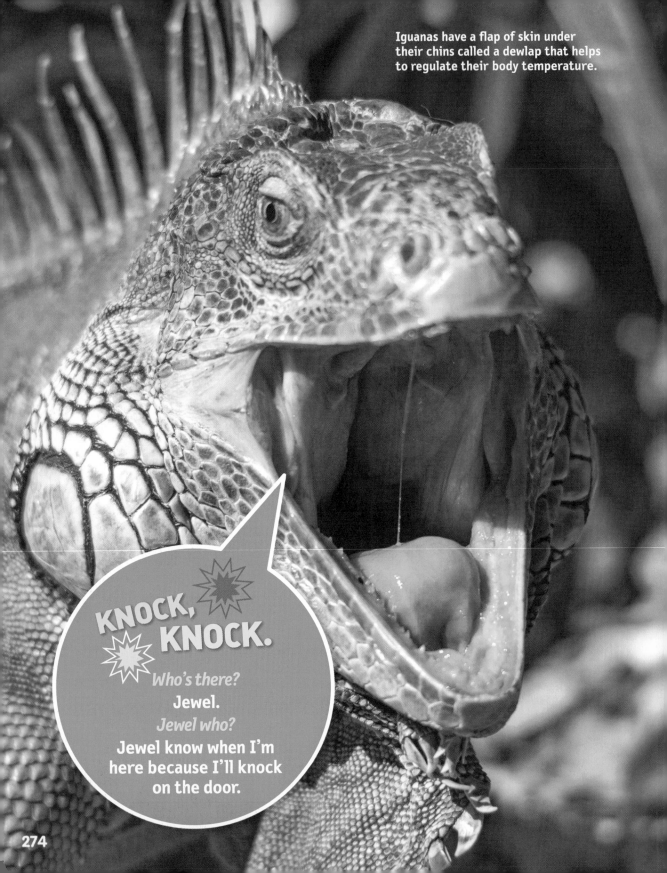

Iguanas have a flap of skin under their chins called a dewlap that helps to regulate their body temperature.

KNOCK, KNOCK.

Who's there?
Jewel.
Jewel who?
Jewel know when I'm here because I'll knock on the door.

274

Say this fast three times:

Pirates slurp soup on the sloop.

Q How much money does a skunk have?

A One scent.

Q What do you call a slug living on a fancy yacht?

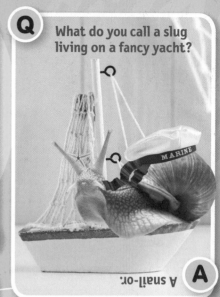

A A snail-or.

Q Why did the queen go to the dentist?

A To get crowns on her teeth.

Q Why did the diamond go to the bathroom?

A Because it had to twinkle.

ARCHAEOLOGIST 1: Wow! Look at these cave paintings we found!
ARCHAEOLOGIST 2: Why did cavemen draw so many pictures of hippopotamuses and rhinoceroses on their walls?
ARCHAEOLOGIST 1: Because they couldn't spell the names.

Q Which bird steals from the rich and gives to the poor?

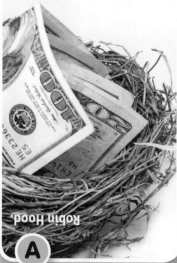

A Robin Hood.

Q Why did the lady buy an **elephant** instead of a **sports car?**

A Because it had a bigger trunk.

Q Why can't a bank keep a secret?

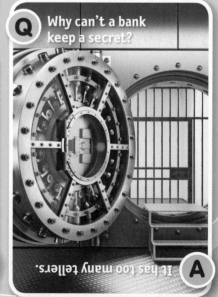

A It has too many tellers.

NAME
Cash

FAVORITE ACTIVITY
Counting my pennies

FAVORITE TOY
Calculator

PET PEEVE
Expired coupons

I CALL MONEY "DOUGH" BECAUSE I KNEAD IT.

I'M GOING TO SPEND THIS AT THE BOOKSTORE ON KITTY LITTER-ATURE.

THE BEST WAY TO SAVE MONEY IS TO FORGET WHO YOU BORROWED IT FROM.

COUNTING MY MONEY MAKES ME PAW-SITIVELY GIDDY.

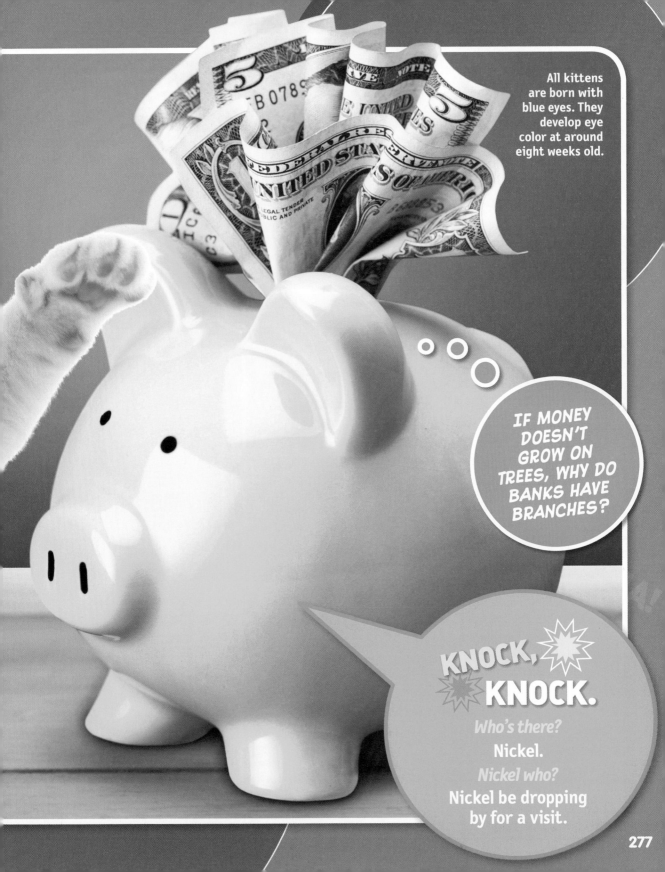

All kittens are born with blue eyes. They develop eye color at around eight weeks old.

IF MONEY DOESN'T GROW ON TREES, WHY DO BANKS HAVE BRANCHES?

KNOCK, KNOCK.

Who's there?

Nickel.

Nickel who?

Nickel be dropping by for a visit.

277

Q Why did the oyster keep all of its pearls?

A Because it was shellfish.

Q Where does a shrimp go to sell his diamond necklace?

A The prawn shop.

Q Why did the pirate buy a new ship?

A Because it was on sail.

A GOLDEN EGG! I'M RICH!

Q Why did the employees bring **swimming trunks** and **tennis racquets** to work?

A Because they were headed to mining camp.

DAD: Have you found a nice card for Mom yet? You've opened 100 of them so far!
DAUGHTER: I know, I'm looking for one with money inside.

HAPPY:) BIRTHDAY

Q What's valuable, **green,** and **sings?**

A Emerald Presley.

JEWELER: How do you feel about these jewels?
CUSTOMER: My love for jewels is crystal clear!

Why did the archaeologist move the Egyptian pyramids closer to the Nile River? **Q**

A So they could have a tomb with a view.

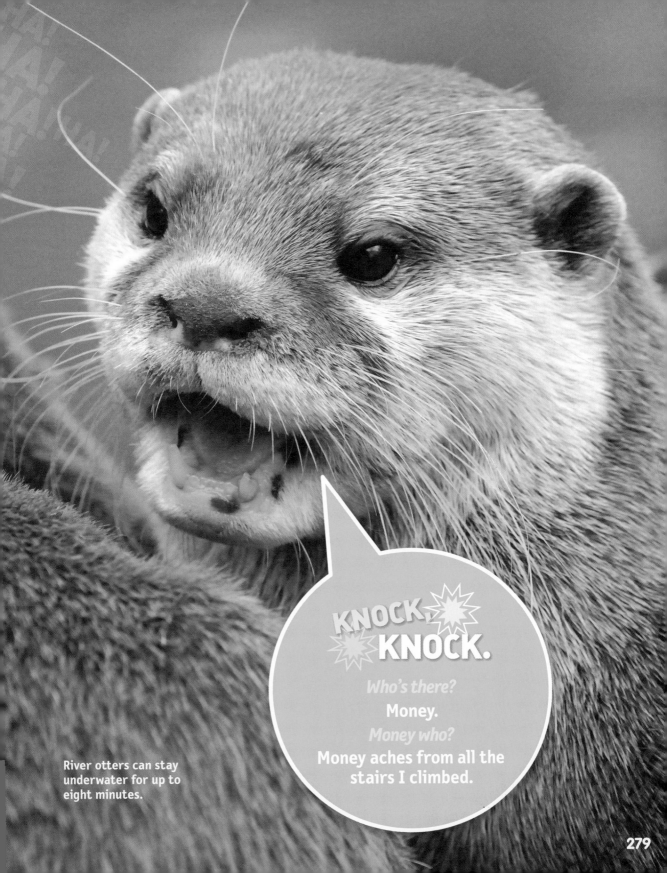

River otters can stay underwater for up to eight minutes.

KNOCK, KNOCK.

Who's there?
Money.
Money who?
Money aches from all the stairs I climbed.

LOL RICHES

The term **"FUNNY MONEY"** describes **COUNTERFEIT,** or fake, **money.**

An orange, **10-foot (3-m)-tall** metal statue of a **balloon dog** sold at auction for **$142 million!**

The first **American coin,** called the **FUGIO CENT,** was designed by **Benjamin Franklin** and was inscribed **"Mind Your Business."**

A man once **PRANKED treasure hunters** by burying a chest filled with **chocolate gold coins** and **costume jewelry.**

A JEWELER IN HONG KONG BUILT A **$27 MILLION BATHROOM.** THE TOILET AND SINK WERE MADE OF SOLID 24-KARAT GOLD.

JOKEFINDER

ILLUSTRATIONCREDITS

Abbreviations: DS = Dreamstime; GI = Getty Images; SS = Shutterstock
Front cover: (UP RT), Pitipat Usanakornkul/SS; (LE), Heinrich van den Berg/GI; (LO RT), Robynrg/SS; **Back cover:** Richard Yoshida/SS; **Spine:** Pitipat Usanakornkul/SS; 1, Seregraff/SS; 2 (UP LE), Grigorita Ko/SS; 2 (UP CTR), Csanad Kiss/SS; 2 (UP RT), photomaster/SS; 2 (CTR LE), Natalia Kirsanova/SS; 2 (CTR), Wiboon Wiratthanaphan/SS; 2 (CTR RT), effective stock photos/SS; 2 (LO LE), Mark O'Flaherty/SS; 2 (LO CTR), Sandra Standbridge/SS; 2 (LO RT), Turbojet/SS; 3 (UP RT), Pitipat Usanakornkul/SS; 3 (CTR LE), Heinrich van den Berg/GI; 3 (LO RT), Robynrg/SS; 4-5, sniper thaphae/SS; 6-7 (BACKGROUND), Aekawut Rattawan/SS; 6 (LO RT), DR Travel Photo and Video/SS; 7 (CTR), Javier Brosch/SS; 8 (UP RT), Kalamurzing/SS; 8 (CTR LE), anna_pro3/SS; 8 (CTR LE), Smit/SS; 8 (LO CTR), Best dog photo/SS; 8 (CTR RT), Elnur/SS; 9 (UP), Blueenayim/DS; 9 (UP CTR LE), (UP CTR), Elnur/SS; 9 (UP RT), Richard Peterson/SS; 9 (CTR), Nadezhda V. Kulagina/SS; 9 (LO LE), FotoYakov/SS; 9 (LO RT), Vyaseleva Elena/SS; 10 (UP LE), Emilia Stasiak/SS; 10 (UP

LE), Draghicich/DS; 10 (UP CTR), David Tadevosian/SS; 10 (UP RT), milart/SS; 10 (UP RT), Winai Tepsuttinun/SS; 10 (CTR LE), Laborant/SS; 10 (CTR LE), Grigorev Mikhail/SS; 10 (CTR RT), Anurak Pongpatimet/SS; 10 (LO LE), Jagodka/SS; 10 (LO CTR), Chaykha.j.s/SS; 10 (LO RT), Africa Studio/SS; 11, Santi Nanta/SS; 12, Grigorita Ko/SS; 13 (UP CTR), Madhourse/SS; 13 (UP CTR RT), Richard Peterson/SS; 13 (UP RT), Robynrg/SS; 13 (CTR RT), Nataliia K/SS; 13 (LO LE), Dora Zett/SS; 13 (LO CTR), Inna Astakhova/SS; 13 (LO RT), Vangert/SS; 14-15, Minerva Studio/SS; 16 (UP LE), vblinov/SS; 16 (UP), Apple's Eyes Studio/SS; 16 (CTR LE), Tsekhmister/SS; 16 (CTR LE), nafterphoto/SS; 16 (CTR RT), Koldunov Alexey/SS; 16 (LO), idreamphoto/SS; 17 (UP LE), Dpullman/DS; 17 (UP CTR), Jan Sommer/SS; 17 (UP RT), Aneta Jungerova/SS; 17 (UP RT), halfmax.ru/SS; 18-19 (BACKGROUND), Trong Nguyen/SS; 18 (LO RT), Mik122/iStockphoto; 19 (UP RT), Tsekhmister/SS; 19 (LO RT), Prokrida/SS; 20, Eric Isselee/SS; 21 (UP LE), (UP RT), Eric Isselee/SS; 21 (UP CTR), Jak Wonderly/NGS; 21 (UP CTR RT), darkpurplebear/SS; 21 (CTR LE), Noor Haswan Noor Azman/

Since 1888, the National Geographic Society has funded more
than 12,000 research, exploration, and preservation projects
around the world. The Society receives funds from National
Geographic Partners, LLC, funded in part by your purchase.
A portion of the proceeds from this book supports this vital
work. To learn more, visit natgeo.com/info.

For more information, visit nationalgeographic.com,
call 1-800-647-5463, or write to the following address:

National Geographic Partners
1145 17th Street N.W.
Washington, D.C. 20036-4688 U.S.A.

Visit us online at nationalgeographic.com/books

For librarians and teachers: ngchildrensbooks.org

More for kids from National Geographic:
natgeokids.com

National Geographic Kids magazine inspires children
to explore their world with fun yet educational articles
on animals, science, nature, and more. Using fresh
storytelling and amazing photography, *Nat Geo Kids*
shows kids ages 6 to 14 the fascinating truth about
the world—and why they should care.
kids.nationalgeographic.com/subscribe

For information about special discounts for bulk
purchases, please contact National Geographic Books
Special Sales: specialsales@natgeo.com

For rights or permissions inquiries, please
contact National Geographic Books Subsidiary
Rights: bookrights@natgeo.com

The publisher would like to thank the following people
for making this book possible: Kate Hale, executive editor;
Michaela Weglinski, editorial assistant; Callie Broaddus,
senior designer; Sarah J. Mock, senior photo editor;
Joan Gossett, editorial production manager; Molly Reid,
production editor; and Anne LeongSon and Gus Tello, design
production assistants.

Design, Editorial, and Production by
Plan B Book Packagers

Trade paperback ISBN: 978-1-4263-3168-8
Reinforced library binding ISBN: 978-1-4263-3169-5

Printed in China
18/RRDS/1